THE ONE THAT DIDN'T GET AWAY

THE ONE THAT DIDN'T GET AWAY

EDITED BY TOM QUINN

Quiller

Copyright © 2024 Tom Quinn

First published in the UK in 2024
by Quiller, an imprint of Amberley Publishing Ltd

British Library Cataloguing-in-Publication Data
A catalogue record for this book is available
from the British Library

ISBN 978-1-84689-401-5 (hardback)
ISBN 978-1-84689-402-2 (e-book)

The right of Tom Quinn to be identified as the author of this work has been asserted in accordance with the Copyright, Design and Patent Act 1988. The information in this book is true and complete to the best of our knowledge. All recommendations are made without any guarantee on the part of the Publisher, who also disclaims any liability incurred in connection with the use of this data or specific details.

All rights reserved. No part of this book may be reproduced or transmitted in any form or by any means, electronic or mechanical including photocopying, recording or by any information storage and retrieval system, without permission from the Publisher in writing.

Cover illustration by John Holder

Typesetting by SJmagic DESIGN SERVICES, India.
Printed in Malta

Quiller

An imprint of Amberley Publishing Ltd
The Hill, Merrywalks, Stroud, GL5 4EP
Tel: 01453 847800
Email: info@quillerbooks.com
Website: www.quillerpublishing.com

As soon as you think of fishing you think of things that don't belong to the modern world. The very idea of sitting all day under a willow tree beside a quiet pool – and being able to find a quiet pool to sit beside – belongs to a time before the war, before radio, before aeroplanes ...
George Orwell, *Coming Up for Air*

The trout within yon wimpling burn
Glides swift, a silver dart,
And, safe beneath the shady thorn,
Defies the angler's art.
James Tayler, *Fly Fishing*, 1888

You that fish for dace and roches,
Carpes or tenches, bonus noches,
Thou wast borne between two dishes,
When the fryday signe was fishes.
Anon

Contents

INTRODUCTION	11

1 HIGH DAYS AND HOLIDAYS

Big Fish, Tiny Fly	12
A Beauty from a Ditch!	14
A Carp on Roach Tackle	15
Brazilian Fishing Dog	20
If They Don't Sleep, They Rises to the Top of the Water: Battles with Mister Conger	22
When the Boulder Came to Life	25
Two Big Salmon on One Cast	28
An Honest Fly-Taker – the Sprightly Dace	29
Remembrance of Things Past	31
Battle Royal – and a Trout Against all the Odds	32
Twelve-Hour Battle with a Salmon	36
The Impossible Fish and the Bluebottle	37
Light Hold on a Thames Giant	39
The Ghostly Twin	42
A Gathering of Giant Pike	44
Mixed Bag to Beat …	47

2 AGAINST THE ODDS

Barbel Landed on a Single Horsehair	48
Beginner's Luck and a Novice Sea Trout	50
A Whopper in the Weir	52
Thames Miracle	55
Salmon on Horsehair and Hazel	58
Nothing Goes Right and Then Nothing Goes Wrong	58

The Last of the Thames Trout	64
A Hopeless Chance …	66
Right up to the Wire	68
The Duck-Eating Golden Pike	69
Three Wild Days in Wessex	71
Christmas Chubbing	77
Just When all Seemed Lost	85
The Most Provoking Loch …	92
An Eel Takes a Trout Fly	96

3 SHOW-STOPPING … AND HEART-STOPPING

Two on at Once	97
What a Battle was This …	100
Not Quite Impossible	102
A Record for the Eden	103
Freaks Fresh from the Sea …	105
Herrings Caught on the Fly	106
Thankless Task	106
Salmon on the Vicar's Side!	108
A Tench Caught on a Fly	109
Definitely an Undeserved Fish	110
An Ancient Fish from the Dark	111
A Giant Pike Lost … and Then Landed	113
The Biter Bit …	123

4 PLEASURES OF THE FISH

Lucky Angler … Very Unlucky Salmon	125
Specimens in the Old Canal	126
Salmon Fishing – Much too Easy!	128
Salmon Enchanted Evening	132
Fought by Firelight – a Fifty-Pounder from the Wye	133

Joey the Impossible Trout, and the Importance of Half-Truths	138
Pike on Bacon	140
Slack-Line Beetling	141
Almost too Easy!	142
Brook Trout in the Jungle	143
Mad, Mad Mayfly	149
A Carp Takes to the Air	152

5 GLORY DAYS

Floods and Storm – and a Fine Fish	156
Battle of a Lifetime	158
Betrayed by a Reel	161
A Grumpy Gillie on the Dee	164
Fish from a Ruined Swim	167
Tied and Tangled	169
Everything Comes to Him who Waits	172
Fly Fishing with a Spinning Rod	175
Bass Gone Mad	177
Never Such Luck Again	180
New Rod, First Salmon	183
Better Wild Than Stocked	188

Introduction

WE – BY which I mean anglers – are a curious bunch. We love to tell tales of the one that got away – the thirty-pound salmon that made a last, mad rush and cut the line on a rock, the huge tench that threw the hook just as it neared the landing net – but we neglect those happier days when the sun shines and we can hardly put a foot wrong.

Of course, the disastrous days are never entirely disastrous because at the very least they whet the appetite for another day by lakeside or riverbank; and we return to fishing each time more determined because each and every outing could be that glorious red-letter day when everything goes to plan and that fish of a lifetime does not get away.

The One That Didn't Get Away celebrates these red-letter days – and for the vast majority of Britain's near one million anglers there are always red-letter days. They may not come thick and fast and they may not involve a fish that breaks all the records, but we have all known the supreme excitement, the joy even, of landing a fish beyond all expectation.

And it was ever thus which is why I have trawled through a vast archive of reports from contemporary sources as well as from long-forgotten angling newspapers and magazines to unearth the most amusing, intriguing and occasionally extraordinary stories of angling at its best – stories that include big fish landed against all the odds on the flimsiest of tackle, monsters netted just when all hope had been lost and wonderful fish brought to the bank in the most unlikely of circumstances.

Whatever your interest in angling, whether you are a game fisher, coarse or sea angler, you will find much here to entertain and to delight – and to remind you why the next best thing to fishing is reading about it!

Chapter 1

HIGH DAYS AND HOLIDAYS

Big Fish, Tiny Fly

THE UPPER part of the back stream at Kimbridge joined the Mottisfont water then rented by our old friends, Foster and Alexander Mortimore.

They asked us to fix a date to come over and have a turn in their water, and the only available day was June 7th. Foster Mortimore wrote to us in a day or two that he was afraid we should be full late as there were few fresh flies hatching. However, we decided to go and chance it.

The rods at Mottisfont that day were the two brothers Mortimore, John Day, Marryat, and myself. On our arrival we found the meadows, and even the railway line, covered with spent gnats, and clouds of males were dancing in the air.

There had been very few sub-imagines hatching on the 6th and at our host's suggestion we decided to try all the wide carriers that held fish.

I do not think we saw a single green drake, and these big fish were as shy as possible, having been fished hard for many days, and a large proportion of them hooked and lost.

Occasionally the female imagines would be seen laying their eggs, and at intervals a fall of spent gnat on the water would bring every fish on the rise.

Presently we had a terrific thunderstorm, and we all took shelter in the station booking office. As soon as it cleared off, we separated, the two Mortimores going downstream, Marryat walking up, and John Day and I having the central part of the water. Day would not fish; he had been hard at it all through the mayfly, and with his usual unselfishness wanted to see me get a big one.

In one of the carriers, we saw the head of a huge trout come up and take a spent gnat. I was on my knees in a moment, crawled up in position and waited for the next rise. This is always a good policy when trout are on spent gnat, as they invariably travel and are dreadfully shy. Up it came again four or five yards higher up, a good underhanded cast landed the fly right at the first attempt, and the fish came with a flop which set my heart beating.

I struck, and upstream went the fish at a great pace. The carrier was full of thick weed beds, and for a time I managed to keep on terms with the trout. At last, it plunged into the thickest part of the vegetation, and worked itself round the weeds until at length it stopped.

In those days we knew nothing of the wonders wrought by slacking a hooked fish, and working it out of the weeds by hand, so I held on and did all I could to move the brute. It was of no avail: Day started off, got hold of a pole and went over to the far side of the carrier and tried to move the weeds apart so that we could get at the trout. The usual result ensued – the trout started, and in a moment broke the gut and was free.

Feeling very downhearted, I tried to persuade Day to have a turn at the next rising fish, but he declined and did his best to console me and held out all sorts of alluring prospects

of another bigger fish higher up the same carrier, and just below a brick bridge. On our arrival at this place, sure enough, the fish was on the rise, and after another ineffectual attempt to get Day to fish it, I repaired the damage and put up another spent gnat.

The trout was rising in a small open space below the bridge, and above another fearful tangle of weed.

Using all care and keeping well out of sight, another horizontal cast put the fly on the spot, another bold rise, and I found myself again in another big fish.

I then did what I should have done with the first one, jumped up, and without a moment's consideration, skull-dragged the trout over the weed bed and started at full pace downstream. After about thirty yards of this the fish shook its head with a savage jerk and tried to turn upstream. I simply stopped it by brute force, and once more started dragging it down as fast as I could go. This was repeated several times, and at last, when we were quite 150 yards below the bridge, the fish made a roll on the water and was netted by Day before it could recover. It was a splendid female and weighed four pounds two ounces.

F. M. Halford, *An Angler's Autobiography*, 1903

A Beauty from a Ditch!

VERY WONDERFUL is the perspective of childhood, which can make a small burn seem greater than rivers in afterlife. There was one burn which I knew intimately from its source to the sea. Much of the upper part was wooded, and it was stony and shallow, till within two miles of its mouth. Here there was for a child another world. There were no trees, the bottom of the burn was of mud or sand, and the channel was full of rustling reeds, with open pools of some depth at intervals.

These pools had a fascination for me, there was something about them which kept me excited with expectation of great events, as I lay behind the reeds, peering through them, and watching the line intently. The result of much waiting was generally an eel, or a small flat fish up from the sea; or now and then a small trout, but never for many years one of the monsters which I was sure must inhabit such mysterious pools. At last, one evening, something heavy really did take the worm. The fish kept deep, played round and round the pool and could not be seen, but I remember shouting to a companion at a little distance, that I had hooked a trout of one pound, and being conscious from the tone of his reply that he didn't in the least believe me, for a trout of one pound was in those days our very utmost limit of legitimate expectation. But soon it lay on the bank – a beauty from little more than a ditch.

Lord Grey of Falloden, *Fly Fishing*, 1899

A Carp on Roach Tackle

FOR PRACTICAL purposes there are big carp and small carp. The latter you may sometimes hope to catch without too great a strain on your capabilities. The former – well, men have been known to catch them, and there are just a few anglers who have caught a good many.

I myself have caught one, and I will make bold to repeat the tale of the adventure as it was told in *The Field* newspaper of July 1, 1911.

The narrative contains most of what I know concerning the capture of big carp. The most important thing in it is the value which it shows to reside in a modicum of good luck.

So far as my experience goes, it is certain that good luck is the most vital part of the equipment of him who would seek to slay big carp . . .

And so to my story. I had intended to begin it in a much more subtle fashion, and only by slow degrees to divulge the purport of it, delaying the finale as long as possible, until it should burst upon a bewildered world like the last crashing bars of the *1812 Overture*.

Now that a considerable section of the daily press has taken cognisance of the event, it is no good my delaying the modest confession that I have caught a large carp. It is true. But it is a slight exaggeration to state that the said carp was decorated with a golden ring bearing a rare inscription of some sort.

Nor was it the weightiest carp ever taken. Nor was it the weightiest carp of the present season. Nor was it the weightiest carp of June 24. Nor did I deserve it. But enough of negation. Let me turn to the story which will explain the whole of it.

To begin with, I very nearly did not go at all because it rained furiously most of the morning. To continue, towards noon the face of the heavens showed signs of clearness and my mind swiftly made itself up that I would go after all. I carefully disentangled the sturdy rod and the strong line, the hooks, and the other matters which had been prepared the evening before, and started armed with roach tackle. The loss of half a day had told me that it was vain to think of big carp. You cannot of course fish for big carp in half a day. It takes a month.

I mention these things by way of explaining why I had never before caught a really big carp, and also why I do not deserve one now. As I have said, I took with me to Cheshunt Lower Reservoir roach tackle, a tin of small worms, and intention to try for perch, with just a faint hope of tench. The natural condition of the water is weed, the accumulated growth of long years. When I visited it for the first time some eight years ago, I could see nothing but weed, and that was in mid-winter. Now, however, the Highbury Anglers, who have rented the reservoir, have done wonders towards making it fishable.

A good part of the upper end is clear, and elsewhere there are pitches cut out which make excellent feeding grounds for fish and angling grounds for men. Prospecting, I soon came to the forked sticks, which have a satisfying significance to the groundbaitless angler.

Someone else had been there before, and the newcomer may perchance reap the benefit of another man's sowing. So, I sat me down on an empty box thoughtfully and began to angle. It is curious how great, in enclosed water especially, is the affinity between small worms and small perch. For two hours I struggled to teach a shoal of small perch that hooks pull them suddenly out of the water.

It was in vain. Izaak Walton must have based his 'wicked of the world' illustration on the ways of small perch.

I had returned about twenty and was gloomily observing my float begin to bob again when a cheery voice, that of Mr R. G. Woodruff, behind me, observed that I ought to catch something in that swim. I had certainly fulfilled the obligation; and it dawned on me that he was not speaking of small perch, and then that my rod was resting on the forked stick and myself on the wood box of the Hon. Secretary of the Anglers' Association. He almost used force to make me stay where I was, but who was I to occupy a place so carefully baited for carp, and what were my insufficient rod and flimsy line that they should offer battle to ten-pounders? Besides, there was tea waiting for me, and I had had enough of small perch.

So I made way for the rightful owner of the pitch, but not before he had given me good store of big lobworms, and

also earnest advice to try for carp with them, roach rod or no roach rod. He told me of a terrible battle of the evening before when a monster took his worm in the dark and also his cast and hook. Whether it travelled north or south he could hardly tell in the gloom but it travelled far and successfully. He hoped that after the rain there might be a chance of a fish that evening.

Finally, I was so far persuaded that during tea I looked out a strong cast and a perch hook on fairly stout gut, and soaked them in the teapot till they were stained a light brown. Then, acquiring a loaf of bread by good fortune, I set out to fish. There were plenty of other forked sticks here and there which showed where other members had been fishing, and I finally decided on a pitch at the lower end, which I remembered from the winter as having been the scene of an encounter with a biggish pike that got off after a considerable fight.

There, with a background of trees and bushes, some of whose branches made handling a fourteen-foot rod rather difficult, it is possible to sit quietly and fairly inconspicuous. And there accordingly I sat for three hours and a quarter, watching a float which only moved two or three times when a small perch pulled the tail of the lobworm, and occupying myself otherwise by making pellets of paste and throwing them out as groundbait.

Though fine it was a decidedly cold evening, with a high wind; but this hardly affected the water, which is entirely surrounded by a high bank and a belt of trees. Nor was there much to occupy the attention except when some great fish would roll over in the weeds far out, obviously one of the big carp, but a hundred yards away. An occasional moorhen and a few rings made by small roach were the only signs of life. The black tip of my float about eight yards away, in the dearth of other interests began to have an almost hypnotising influence. A little after half past eight this tip trembled and then disappeared and so intent was I on looking at it that my first thought was a mild wonder as to why it did that. Then the coiled line began to go through the rings, and I realised that here was a bite.

Rod in hand, I waited until the line drew taut, and struck gently.

Then things became confused. It was as though some submarine suddenly shot out into the lake. The water was about six feet deep, and the fish must have been near the bottom, but he made a most impressive wave as he dashed straight into the weeds about twenty yards away, and buried himself in them. And so home, I murmured to myself, or words to that effect, for I saw not the slightest chance of getting a big fish out with a roach rod and fine line. After a little thought, I decided to try hand-lining, as one does for trout, and getting hold of the line – with some difficulty because the trees prevented the rod point going far back – I proceeded to feel for the fish with my hand.

At first there was no response; the anchorage seemed immovable.

Then I thrilled to a movement at the other end of the line which gradually increased until the fish was on the run again, pushing the weeds aside as he went, but carrying a great streamer or two with him on the line. His run ended, as had the first, in another weed patch, and twice after he seemed to have found safety in the same way. Yet each time hand-lining was efficacious, and eventually I got him into the strip of clear water; here the fight was an easier affair, though by no means won.

It took, I suppose, some fifteen or twenty minutes before I saw a big bronze side turn over, and was able to get about half the fish into my absurdly small net. Luckily by this time he had no fight left in him, and I dragged him safely up the bank and fell upon him. What he weighed I had no idea, but I put him at about twelve pounds, with a humble hope that he might be more.

At any rate, he had made a fight that would have been considered very fair in a twelve-pound salmon, the power of

his runs being certainly no less and the pace of them quite as great. On the tackle I was using, however, a salmon would have fought longer.

The fish in my net, I was satisfied, packed up my tackle, and went off to see what the other angler had done. So far, he had not had a bite, but he meant to go on as long as he could see, and hoped to meet me at the train. He did not do so, for a very good reason; he was at that moment engaged in a grim battle in the darkness with a fish that proved ultimately to be one ounce heavier than mine, which, weighed on the scales at the keeper's cottage, was sixteen pounds five ounces. As I owe him my fish, because it was his advice that I put on the strong cast, and the bait was one of his lobworms, he might fairly claim the brace. And he would deserve them, because he is a real carp fisher and has taken great pains to bring about his success. For myself – well, luck attends the undeserving now and then. One of them has the grace to be thankful.

H. T. Sheringham, *Coarse Fishing*, 1912

Brazilian Fishing Dog

ONE DAY I witnessed a very strange thing, the action of a dog by the waterside. It was evening and the beach was forsaken; cartmen, boatmen, fishermen, all gone, and I was the only idler left on the rocks; but the tide was coming in, rolling quite big waves on to the rocks, and the novel sight of the waves, the freshness, the joy of it, kept me at that spot, standing on one of the outermost rocks not yet washed over by the water.

By and by a gentleman, followed by a big dog, came down to the beach and stood at a distance of forty or fifty yards from me, while the dog bounded forward over the flat, slippery rocks and through pools of water until he came to my side, and sitting on the edge of the rock began gazing intently down at the water.

He was a big, shaggy, round-headed animal, with a greyish coat with some patches of light reddish colour on it; what his breed was I cannot say, but he looked somewhat like a sheepdog or an otterhound. Suddenly he plunged in, quite vanishing from sight, but quickly reappeared with a big shad of about three and a half to four pounds weight in his jaws.

Climbing on to the rock he dropped the fish, which he had not appeared to have injured much, as it began floundering about in an exceedingly lively manner. I was astonished and looked back at the dog's master; but there he stood in the same place, smoking and paying no attention to what his animal was doing.

Again, the dog plunged in and brought out a second big fish and dropped it on the flat rock, and again and again he dived, until there were five big shads all floundering about on the wet rock and likely soon to be washed back into the water.

The shad is a common fish in the Plata and the best to eat of all its fishes, resembling the salmon in its rich flavour, and is eagerly watched for when it comes up from the sea by the Buenos Aires fishermen, just as our fishermen watch for mackerel on our coasts.

But on this evening the beach was deserted by everyone, watcher included, and the fish came and swarmed along the rocks, and there was no one to catch them – not even some poor hungry idler to pounce and carry off the five fishes the dog had captured. One by one I saw them washed back into the water, and presently the dog, hearing his master whistling him, bounded away.

W. H. Hudson, *Far Away and Long Ago*, 1918

If They Don't Sleep, They Rises to the Top of the Water: Battles with Mister Conger

AT LAST, the weather became favourable. We therefore at once determined to go fishing, and see whether, after their long holiday from hook and line the fish would not be in a biting humour.

'How long shall we be out?' said the friend who went with me.

'As long as the fish bite,' said I, 'therefore we had better take some food with us, for there are no bakers' shops by the Spit Buoy, and they don't sell cheese at the Boyne.'

'Morning, sir,' said Barney, the civil and obliging provider of boats on the beach, and whose name was once Barnabas, but who never will be called anything but Barney again. 'Better have the *Laughing Jackass*, sir, she's all ready.'

I have an unfortunate habit of looking after little matters, and knowing that there is a hole, which ought to be stopped up by a cork in the bottom of every boat, I examined it to see if the cork was in its place; of course it was not. We soon got a cork and fastened it in tight, one of our party telling us that he once knew a young man who went out a little way to sea, and who, finding that there was a little water in the bottom of the boat, actually took the cork out of the hole to let the water out, quite forgetting that the water would rush in; it did rush in to his great surprise, and the boat was pretty nearly full before he could get ashore again.

We were soon out on the marks Robinson Crusoe had indicated, and were wondering whether the old man would keep his appointment. At last, we were delighted to see him paddling away out of the harbour. He was soon alongside, his brave old face radiant with smiles, for he had taken a great fancy to me, though he does not to everybody.

'Are we on the marks, George?'

'Not by a long ways, sir.'

'Then just put us right like a good fellow, will you? Better come into our boat; we will tow your old tub astern.'

'Don't you go to insult my old boat, sir, or I won't show you the wrack.'

'Never mind, George, it's only a joke.'

'Let go the anchor, boy,' said George.

The boy picked it up and spat on it.

'What's that for?' said I.

'That's for luck,' said George. 'And to make the fish bite; but it don't always, for a chap the other day spit on his anchor (and it was a brannew one, too) he heaved it overboard; but there was no cable on it so he lost it right off, and was obliged to go home to fetch another, so he lost his anchor and his tide of fish too.'

'When do you go out fishing most, George?'

'I don't fish much of a day, sir; I fishes at night most and almost every night too when it's anyways like weather. I got no clock nor yet watch; but I've got the stars, as will let me know the time to a quarter of an hour. There's one star in particular as serves me, and in a month's time I noticed there was never a quarter of an hour's difference in her time.'

'Do you ever go to sleep, George?'

'No, sir. I don't go to sleep; but I tell you what, sir, I thinks the fish sleep of nights that's my experience of them. I've been out thousands of nights and I've always observed as one particular hour is different from any other hour of a night, and that's between twelve and one.

'The fish never bites at that time, and after that hour is over they begins again and keeps on till daylight; but before that hour they always fishes slack, and I can sleep between twelve and one if I likes, for it's no use heaving the line overboard; but after the clock strikes one the fish won't let me go to sleep and I've always found it so.

'That's what makes me think the fish sleep; if they don't sleep they rises to the top of the water. When the water is thick and it's a moonlight night, that's the time to catch 'em if the water is thick and it's dark too, the fish can't see the bait. They are on the bite, too, of frosty nights. I puts my sail over my head, and it gets as white as a sheet. I often prays for it not to come daylight, for I never feels cold as long as the fish bites, the night is the best time to catch the congers, sir. The congers is as taffety fish as is; there's not a delicater fish as swims, and they are very nice in their feeding. If a whelk was to get on the bait the conger would never touch it, not if you was to bid at right; they are regular bait robbers them whelks. But when the congers gets on to the hook they lets you know it, and when you pulls them up, they curls their tails and holds a powerful sight of water; it's ten to one you don't lose them if you have not got strong gear. But you must have nice fresh bait.

'If there's a bone in the bait, they won't touch it; Master Conger will have the first grab, or none at all. I've cut up a dozen pouts, and seen the conger whack at them all, and then he never takes them if they don't quite suit his taste. The biggest conger as ever I catched was in the grass at the back of the Gosport Hospital. Just as the sun goes down I hooks my gentleman, and says I to the man who was fishing near me: "Joe, I've got him this time and no mistake, and a beautiful fish he is!"

'He towed me and my little boat round my anchor six times, and I got a good Dutch line, so strong that three men could not break it, for we tried it afterwards. Master Conger had got hooked outside of his teeth, still the hook had a good strong hold, but yet it gave him the chance of chawing the line; and he kept on chawing it a good one, so I played him till at last I got him alongside, and tried to haul him, and then he flew right at me out of the water. It was a terrible dark night, and I could hardly see, but I hit him a rap over the head with my stump, and then I was obliged to let him run again, or he would have slewed my arm right off, and pulled me out of the boat as well, for I could not slip my cable. At last, I got terribly tired, and so did Master Conger, for he let me haul him up alongside; Joe then came up with his boat, and we both whipped into him amidships, and jerked him into the boat. When he got aboard I thought he would have knocked my old boat all to pieces, for he was fore and aft in a minute, and sent everything flying. I was only afraid he would get his tail on the gunwale (for congers is terribly strong in the tail) and then he would have hauled himself overboard; so I watched my chance, and hit him a crack just where his life lay, and then he was quiet at last.

'He was all six foot long and sixteen inches round the thickest part.

'His great head was like a sheep's, and his jaws was awful. I sold over four shillings' worth of him, besides what I ate myself; and all along his backbone was fat, as fine and white as suet.

'He was a fish he was.'

Frank Buckland, *Curiosities of Natural History*, 1858

When the Boulder Came to Life

THE THIRD day, in the afternoon, we had our first and only thorough sensation in the shape of a big trout. It came none too soon. The interest had begun to flag. But one big fish a week will do. It is a pinnacle of delight in the angler's experience that he may well be three days in working up to, and once reached, it is three days down to the old humdrum level again. At least it is with me.

It was a dull, rainy day; the fog rested low upon the mountains, and the time hung heavily on our hands. About

three o'clock the rain slackened and we emerged from our den, Joe going to look after his horse, which had eaten but little since coming into the woods, the poor creature was so disturbed by the loneliness and the black flies; I, to make preparations for dinner, while my companion lazily took his rod and stepped to the edge of the big pool in front of camp. At the first introductory cast, and when his fly was not fifteen feet from him on the water, there was a lunge and a strike, and apparently the fisherman had hooked a boulder. I was standing a few yards below engaged in washing out the coffee pail, when I heard him call out: 'I have got him now!'

'Yes, I see you have,' said I, noticing his bending pole and moveless line.

'When I am through I will help you get loose.'

'No, but I'm not joking,' he said. 'I have got a big fish.' I looked up again, but saw no reason to change my impression and kept on with my work.

It is proper to say that my companion was a novice at fly fishing, he never having cast a fly until this trip.

Again he called out to me, but deceived by his coolness and nonchalant tones, and by the lethargy of the fish, I gave little heed. I knew very well that if I had struck a fish that held me down in that way I should have been going through a regular war dance on that circle of boulder-tips, and should have scared the game into activity, if the hook had failed to wake him up. But as the farce continued, I drew nearer.

'Does that look like a stone or a log?' said my friend, pointing to his quivering line, slowly cutting the current up toward the centre of the pool.

My scepticism vanished in an instant, and I could hardly keep my place on the top of the rock.

'I can feel him breathe,' said the now warming fisherman, 'just feel of that pole.'

I put my eager hand upon the butt and could easily imagine I felt the throb or pant of something alive down there in the black depths.

But whatever it was it moved like a turtle. My companion was praying to hear his reel spin, but it gave out now and then only a few hesitating clicks. Still the situation was excitingly dramatic, and we were all actors. I rushed for the landing net, but being unable to find it, shouted desperately for Joe, who came hurrying back, excited before he had learned what the matter was.

The net had been left at the lake below, and must be had with the greatest dispatch.

In the meantime, I skipped from boulder to boulder as the fish worked this way or that about the pool, peering into the water to catch a glimpse of him, for he had begun to yield a little to the steady strain that was kept upon him. Presently I saw a shadowy, unsubstantial something just emerge from the black depths, then vanish. Then I saw it again, and this time the huge proportions of the fish were faintly outlined by the white facings of his fins. The sketch lasted but a twinkling; it was only a flitting shadow upon a darker background, but it gave me the profoundest Izaak Walton thrill I ever experienced. I had been a fisher from my earliest boyhood. I came from a race of fishers; trout streams gurgled about the roots of the family tree, and there was a long accumulated and transmitted tendency and desire in me that that sight gratified. I did not wish the pole in my own hands; there was quite enough electricity overflow from it and filling the air for me. The fish yielded more and more against the relentless pressure of the rod, till, in about fifteen minutes, from the time he was hooked, he came to the surface, then made a little whirlpool where he disappeared again. But presently he was up a second time and lashing the water into foam as the angler led him towards the rock upon which I was perched, net in hand. As I reached towards him, off he went again, and taking another circle of the pool, came up still more ready for the net, when, between his rages, I carefully ran the net under him and lifted him ashore, amid, it is needless to say, the wildest enthusiasm of the spectators.

'What does he weigh?' was the natural enquiry of each; and we took it in turns hefting him. But gravity was less potent

to us then than usual, and the fish seemed astonishingly light after such a battle.

Four pounds, we said, but Joe said more. So, we improvised a scale; a long strip of board was balanced across a stick, and our groceries served as weights. A four-pound package of sugar kicked the beam quickly; a pound of coffee was added; still it went up; then a pound of tea, and still the fish had a little of the best of it. But we called it six pounds, not to drive too sharp a bargain with fortune, and were more than satisfied. Such a beautiful creature, marked in every respect like a trout of six inches. We feasted our eyes upon him for half an hour. We stretched him upon the ground and admired him, we laid him across a log and withdrew a few paces to admire him, we hung him against the shanty and turned our heads from side to side as women do when they are selecting dress-goods, the better to take in the full force of the effect.

John Burroughs, *Locusts and Wild Honey*, 1879

Two Big Salmon on One Cast

MR G. Robinson, of Seal House, Hexham, when fishing in Alnwick Grange Water on Saturday last, almost simultaneously hooked two salmon.

The dropper fly was first taken by a fish apparently of fourteen or fifteen pounds which took the fly near the surface of the water and on going down with it brought the stretcher fly to the surface when a larger fish sprang out of the water and seized it.

Both fish ran a considerable distance up the stream when the one at the stretcher repeatedly leapt out of the water, making each time a complete somersault, being pulled back, head first, by the other fish. In such a situation it is almost unheard of to avoid losing both fish.

But when they turned back, running down the water, the one on the dropper got free and Mr Robinson joyfully exclaimed: 'I will get the larger one.' The larger fish, after a struggle of twenty-minutes duration was brought to the side and was successfully netted by a gentleman who was fortunately present at the time. The fish was subsequently measured by a member of the Hexham Angling Club and found to be thirty-nine inches long, eighteen and a half inches round and weighed nineteen pounds.

The Field, March, 1870

An Honest Fly-Taker – the Sprightly Dace

I SHOULD be the most ungrateful of anglers if I did not acknowledge my indebtedness to the dace.

It so happened that, whatever else fortune denied me, it gave me opportunities, of which I could without hardship avail myself, for dace fishing; and, whatever sins of omission I may in my old age have to bring forward in self-accusation, I shall never be able to plead guilty to neglecting any opportunities soever in the matter of angling. For the dace, therefore, as a fish whose merits I have appreciated from youth upwards, I entertain great respect.

There is no dullness about it. Go down to the fords where the dace are gathered, and you shall see the water boiling with their gambols, and shooting silver as they wheel and frisk about. Take them under any circumstances, so

long as they are in season, and they always impress you with their liveliness of character. The roach in biting sometimes scarcely moves the quill float; the dace startles you by its sudden, sharp onslaught. A roach firmly hooked ought never to be lost; it requires a dexterous hand to pilot a dace safely out of a rapid current – that is to say, a dace of two or three to the pound.

And the dace is deserving of respect because it will honestly take the fly. True, the roach does so too, occasionally; but the dace, any time between June and September, rises regularly. We used to get them in the Colne considerably over half a pound in weight, and an afternoon's perseverance and a little wading would, in favourable weather, put from twenty to thirty fish into your landing net. But it is questionable whether this can be done now.

Many a pleasant evening have I spent by Thames-side, beginning at Ham Lane and working upwards, or crossing the river below Richmond Bridge; fishing always with fine tackle and a black gnat somewhere on the cast.

The finest bit of sport I had with dace was in a mill stream a couple of miles out of Norwich. It was specially welcome because quite unexpected. We were on a pike-fishing excursion, and the fly rod was put into the dog cart to provide bait for the party. The great mill wheel was revolving, and the pool swirling and foaming, when we arrived, and a few small fish could be detected in the shallow water. The general outlook was not inviting, but the apparatus was put together on the chance of things proving better than they looked. Chance favoured us. The first cast produced a dace on each hook, and in a quarter of an hour I had whipped out a good supply of bait for the trollers and spinners. So long as the dace were rising all the pike in the river could not tempt me to accompany them. I stuck to the fly, and only left off when I was too tired to wield the rod any more.

William Senior, Lines in Pleasant Places, 1920

Remembrance of Things Past

I REMEMBER my first visit to Grantley very well when I was about twelve years of age. The keeper met us on a road somewhere above the lake and we walked down marvellous paths carpeted with pine needles to the boathouse. I remember I had a huge creel with me and the keeper remarked jokingly that it was a pity I hadn't brought another basket or two as my creel wouldn't hold what I was likely to catch. He never said anything more true in his life. It was a thundery sort of day and we had several heavy showers and got beautifully wet, but no thunder seemed to stop the Grantley trout. Being twelve years of age, I kept an exact count in my head of the number of trout caught. I started fishing at about eleven o'clock (incidentally, I caught three nice trout from the bank while the keeper was getting the boat ready) and ended the day wet and happy at about seven o'clock. I caught exactly eighty-six trout and they must have averaged at least half a pound: of these we kept forty really lovely trout, the biggest about one and a half pounds. It is a long time ago now, that day, but I can still smell the wet bracken and hear the drone of the thunder showers on the high trees and feel the rod bending, almost continuously, all day. I have fished at Grantley since then but have never had quite such a perfect day. There is rather more weed nowadays and I don't think the trout average quite as big as formerly, but that may be just the difference between twelve years of age and fifty.

George Brennand, Halcyon, 1947

Battle Royal – and a Trout Against all the Odds

THOSE WHO fish rivers where mayfly come will agree that, though with it you get a higher average weight, yet actually the biggest fish are caught on the sedge. 1903 on the Kennet was a great mayfly season for heavy fish, and a friend of mine who had the Ramsbury water got the truly remarkable bag of six fish in one day which weighed over nineteen pounds: and yet the two heaviest fish of the year were got on the sedge. I got the heaviest. It was the 26 July, a cloudy, gusty day, with a downstream wind, and I was on the water from eleven till five without seeing a rise. My friend and I then had tea and walked up the river at a quarter past six. Olives began to appear and trout to move; and suddenly a really large one started rising. We stood and watched, with growing excitement. He was taking every fly, in solid and determined fashion, and the oftener he appeared the bigger he looked, and the faster beat our hearts. It was settled that I was to try for him. I was nervous and uncomfortable. He was very big: it was a long throw and the wind horrible: I could not reach him, and like a fool I got rattled and pulled off too much line: there was an agonised groan from my friend behind me when a great curl of it was slapped on the water exactly over the trout's nose. We looked at each other without speaking, and he silently walked away up the river, leaving me staring stupidly at the spot where the trout had been rising. Of course, he was gone.

The next two hours can be passed over. The small fly rise came and went. I caught a trout on a No. 2 silver sedge and finally, at about a quarter past eight, found myself gazing gloomily at the place where I had bungled. The wild wind had blown itself out and had swept the sky bare of cloud. Silence had come, and stillness. The willows, which all through the long summer day had bowed and chattered in the wind, were straightened and motionless, each individual leaf hanging down as though carved in jade: the forest of great sedges, which the gusts had swept into wave after wave of a roaring sea of emerald, was now calm and level, each stalk standing straight and stiff as on a Japanese screen.

There had occurred that transition, that transmutation from noise and movement to silence and peace, which would be more wonderful were we not so accustomed to it, when a windy summer day turns over to a moveless summer night: when the swing and clatter and rush of the day is arrested and lifted from the world, and you get the sense that the great hollow of the air is filled with stillness and quiet, as with a tangible presence.

They are peaceful things, these summer evenings after wild days, and I remember particularly that this was one of the most peaceful; more so indeed than my thoughts, which were still in a turmoil. I stood watching mechanically, and then, tempting fate to help me, made a cast or two over the spot where the fish had been.

How easy it was to reach it now, how lightly my fly settled on the water, how gracefully it swung over the place. All to no purpose, of course, for nothing happened, and I was about to reel up when a fish rose ten yards above, close under my bank. It was one of those small movements difficult to place. It might be a very large fish or a very small one. A wild thought swept through me that this was my big one: but no, I said to myself, it cannot be. This is not where he was rising. Besides, things do not happen like that, except in books: it is only in books that you make a fearful bungle and go back later and see a small break which you think is a dace, and cast carelessly and hook something the size of an autumn salmon: it is only in books that fate works in such fashion. Why, I know it all so well that I could write it out by heart, every move of it. But this is myself by a river, not reading in a chair. This is the real world, where such things do not happen: that is the rise of a half-pound trout.

I cast. I was looking right into the west, and the water was coloured like skimmed milk by reflection from where the sun had set. My silver sedge was as visible as by day. It floated down, there was a rise, I struck, and something rushed upstream. Then I knew. Above me was open water for some twenty-five yards, and above that again a solid block of weed, stretching right across. My fish made for this, by short, irresistible runs. To let him get into it would have been folly: he must be stopped: either he is well hooked or lightly, the gut is either sound or rotten: kill or cure, he must be turned, if turned he can be: so I pulled hard, and fortunately got his head round and led him down. He played deep and heavy and I had to handle him roughly, but I brought him down with a smash, and I began to breathe again. But then another terror appeared. In the place we had reached the only clear water was a channel under my bank, and the rest of the river was choked with weed.

Should I try to pull him down this channel, about three or four yards wide, to the open water below? No. It was much too dangerous, for the fish was uncontrollable, and if he really wanted to get to weed he would either get there or break me: even with a beaten fish it would be extremely risky, and with an unbeaten one it was unthinkable.

Well, if he would not come down, he must go up, and up he went willingly enough, for when I released pressure he made a long rush up to the higher weed bed, whilst I ran up the meadow after him, and with even greater difficulty turned him once more. This time I thought he was really going right through it, so fast and so heavy was his pull, and I think he was making for a hatch hole above: but once more my gallant gut stood the strain and, resisting vigorously, he was led down again. This proceeding was repeated either two or three times more, I forget which: either three or four times we fought up and down that twenty-five yards of river.

By then he was tiring, and I took up my station in the middle of the stretch, where I hoped to bring him in: my hand was actually on the sling of the net when he suddenly awoke and rushed up. He reached the weed bed at a pace at which it was impossible to stop, shot into it like a torpedo, and I had the sickening certainty that I should lose him after all. To hold him hard now would be to make a smash certain, so I slacked off: when he stopped, I tightened again, expecting miserably to feel the dead, lifeless drag of a weeded line. Instead, to my delight, I found I was still in contact with the fish, and he was pulling hard. How he had carried the line through the weeds I do not know. To look at it seemed impossible . . . But the line was clear, and the fish proved it by careering wildly on towards the hatch, making the reel sing. I believe he meant to go through into the carrier, as fish have done before and after, but I turned him. However, we could not stay where we were.

The hatch was open at the bottom, there was a strong draw of water through it, and if a heavy, beaten fish got into this, no gut would hold him up. At all risks he must be taken over the weed into the clear water. I pulled him up to the top and ran him down. Then, for the first time after so many perils, came the conviction that I should land him. He was obviously big, but how big could not be known, for I had not had a clear sight of him yet. He still pulled with that immovable, quivering solidity only shown by a very heavy fish. But at last even his great strength tired. He gave a wobble or two, yielded and suddenly he was splashing on the top, looking huge in the dusk.

There ensued that agonising time when you have a big fish nearly beat, but he is still too heavy to pull in, and nothing you can do gets him up to the net.

At last, I pulled him over to it, but I lifted too soon, the ring caught in the middle of the body, he wavered a moment in the air and then toppled back into the water with a sickening splash. A judgement, I thought, and for a shattering second I believed he had broken the gut, but he was still on. I was pretty well rattled by then and, in the half light, made two more bad shots, but the end came at last, he was in the net and on the bank.

> How big was he? Three pounds? Yes, and more. Four pounds? Yes, and more. Five? He might be, he might. My knees shook and my fingers trembled as I got him on the scales. He weighed a fraction over four pounds eight ounces.
>
> J. W. Hills, *A Summer on the Test*, 1924

Twelve-Hour Battle with a Salmon

IN THE month of July, some thirty years ago, one Duncan Grant, a shoemaker by profession, who was more addicted to fishing than to his craft, went up the way from the village of Aberlour, in the north, to take a cast in some of the pools above Elchies Water.

He had no great choice of tackle, as may be conceived; nothing, in fact, but what was useful, and scant supply of that. Duncan tried one or two pools without success, till he arrived at a very deep and rapid stream, facetiously termed the Mountebank: here he paused, as if meditating whether he should throw his line or not. 'She is very big,' said he to himself, 'but I'll try her; if I grip him he'll be worth the hauding.'

He then fished it, a step and a throw, about halfway down, when a heavy splash proclaimed that he had raised him, though he missed the fly. Going back a few paces, he came over him again, and hooked him. The first tug verified to Duncan his prognostication, that if he was there, he would be worth the hauding; but his tackle had thirty plies of hair next the fly, and he held fast, nothing daunted. Give and take went on with dubious advantage, the fish occasionally sulking.

The thing at length became serious; and, after a succession of the same tactics, Duncan found himself at the Boat of Aberlour, seven hours after he had hooked his fish, the said fish fast under a stone, and himself completely tired. He had some thoughts of breaking his tackle and giving the thing up; but he finally hit upon an expedient to rest himself, and at the same time to guard against the surprise and consequence of a sudden movement of the fish.

He laid himself down comfortably on the bank, the butt end of his rod in front; and most ingeniously drew out part of his line, which he held in his teeth. 'If he tugs when I'm sleeping,' said he, 'I think I'll find him noo'; and no doubt it is probable he would. Accordingly, after a comfortable nap of three or four hours, Duncan was awoken by a most unceremonious tug at his jaws. In a moment he was on his feet, his rod well up, and the fish swattering down the stream. He followed as best he could, and was beginning to think of the rock at Craigellachie, when he found to his great relief that he could 'get a pull on him'. He had now comparatively easy work; and exactly twelve hours after hooking him, he landed him at the head of Lord Fife's water: he weighed fifty-four pounds and had the tide lice still upon him.

William Scrope, *Days and Nights of Salmon Fishing in the Tweed*, 1843

The Impossible Fish and the Bluebottle

HE WAS an old and wise fish, and had his headquarters opposite a clubhouse on a certain famous stream. Many a fly had passed over his venerable head.

Once long ago it is said that he was hooked on a piece of bread, but quickly wound the line round a stump, extracted the hook and was rising to some natural flies half an hour later. New members used to bet that they would catch him. The old members took their bets and their money and obtained satisfaction out of the fish that way. It was an aggravating feature in that trout's behaviour that nothing would put him down short of a cart rope thrown over his head. He was as tame as a pug dog, but had the cunning, without the wildness, of a hawk.

One day there joined the club a man who was not an expert with the fly rod. He, like the rest, said he thought he could catch the trout. The old members laughed and took his bets, as was their custom with newcomers. A mean thing this, but very much the way of the world.

It was August. One sultry evening the new member came to the club armed with a pea-shooter and many bluebottles. Was he going to catch the trout with a pea-shooter? No; he was only going to begin to catch him – the operation might take some time. Deftly a half-dead bluebottle was puffed out of the tube in front of the fish. It was taken, of course, as everything eatable from a trout's point of view was taken. The fish had a rare supper that evening.

The following day the new member repeated the operation. He fed the fish in this manner for more than a week; the others smiled and looked on.

'I will catch him soon,' said the new member. 'I am only waiting for the right wind.'

At the end of three weeks there came a day when a stiff breeze was blowing upstream. It was the day on which the catastrophe was fated to happen. The new member appeared at the clubhouse with a long slender rod, on which was arranged running tackle and a length of fine, but strong gut, terminating with a single hook.

He took his stand some distance below the fish, and began feeding him as usual. On the hook was a bluebottle.

Good luck helped our friend who, however, exhibited considerable skill. The upstream breeze took the hooked fly just over the trout, and the new member let it fall and at the same time puffed out a fly from the tube.

Which would the trout take? It was an anxious moment. Had the rod been in front instead of behind him, he would have taken neither. But he did not see the rod, having no eyes in his tail (this has been questioned) and the fly containing the hook was sucked in.

How he fought! Was the wisdom of twenty years to culminate in destruction by means of a pea-shooter and a bluebottle? Where was that invaluable stump? The new member had removed it. The weeds? They had been recently cut. A leap for liberty then? That made matters worse for the gut got wound round his body and hampered him sadly. But let fall the curtain. He was landed – as wise and grand and noble a specimen as has ever been seen in a trout stream.

John Bickerdyke, Days of My Life, 1895

Light Hold on a Thames Giant

THE USUAL feeding ground of the big trout was in the blackwater between two runs, just above the lower bay of the weir, and a bright artificial bleak a few inches in length having been deftly arranged so as to spin very rapidly, I took up my place in the punt. Rosewell meanwhile, was mounted on the beam of the weir prospecting about with another spinner, on the chance of coming across another prowling fish.

I proceeded to spin steadily backwards and forwards and up and down the two runs and the intervening wedge of black water, and just as a distant church clock struck seven o'clock, as

I was drawing my bait up to the apron of the weir, a number of small fry flew in all directions, and a rush through the water indicated the presence of the fish we were trying for. I let my spinner gently down, and was drawing it across the stream, when a faint tap made me imagine that a perch or a chub had run at it.

In far less time than it has taken to read these words I struck firmly, my reel was flying round, and a heavy fish plunged at a great rate right down and through the broken white water of the run. It took about forty yards of line in this rush, and then jumped into the air, showing us the outline of a noble trout.

The fish then bored deep in the water and tore across the runs towards the upper end of the weir. Meanwhile, Rosewell, who had, of course, seen what had occurred, stepped into the punt and quietly worked it along the weir to the bay at the lower end, and then to the bank. I got out, and steadying the fish, found it close under the piles of the weir.

On the bank there stood a tree just at the lower end of the weir and I had to lower my rod to pass it round. As I did this the trout made a rush towards me, and although I gathered in the line by hand as rapidly as possible, there was a good deal of slack. To my horror, on recovering this, I found that the line was foul of a willow which grew in the angle of the bay. The position was a desperate one, but Rosewell proved equal to the occasion. Landing net in hand, he stepped into the water and walked down the slippery slope, over which a strong stream was flowing. I trembled, imagining that he intended to try to net the fish, but his judgement was too good for that. Steadying himself with the handle of the

landing net, he took out his knife, opened it, and stooping down, cut away the part of the willow round which the line was foul. As it came clear I raised my rod, and obtaining a good pull at the fish, it started across the weir, and again flung itself into the air.

The rest was dogged, the trout kept boring down and plunging heavily, while at every favourable opportunity I reeled in and held him fast. At last, the plucky fish came to the surface, and just as it rolled over on its side the sun peeped out of the clouds and revealed to our eyes as fair a sight as ever appeared to a fisherman.

In a very few moments it was in the net and on the bank and both Rosewell and I fairly fell upon it for fear of its jumping back into the water. A more perfect specimen of a Thames trout I never saw, although I have seen larger ones.

Before Rosewell extracted the hook from its mouth, we made an examination of the manner in which the fish was hooked. It may have been purely accidental, or it may have pointed the efficacy of weighting our spinners, but whatever it was that fish was held by a single hook which had only the weakest hold.

At this moment a local angler came through the lock in his punt and joined us at the side of the weir. He was naturally sorrowful at our being on the spot before him, but he, in true sportsmanlike spirit, conveyed his warmest congratulations, and insisted on us sampling a curious homemade liquor to drink the health of all good fishermen. After a brief consultation I decided to take the trout down to Halliford in the canoe and get it accurately weighed. On my arrival at the Ship Hotel the landlord put it into the scales and it registered nine pounds. As it was the largest I had hooked and landed, it was despatched to London the same day, and the work of setting it up in a case entrusted to, and most admirably carried out by, the far-famed Mr Cooper.

F. M. Halford, *An Angler's Autobiography*, 1903

The Ghostly Twin

ATLANTIC SALMON are strange creatures. For centuries no one knew where they went when they left our rivers; no one knew that once in freshwater they do not feed at all, but merely snap (if we are lucky) at the angler's fly or spinner out of some old sea-borne habit.

But the salmon's evolutionary niche meant that until the nets-men got going, it was one of the most successful creatures on the planet. Feeding at sea and reproducing in freshwater produced an astonishing abundance of salmon in rivers across the world. So cheap was salmon that legend has it that in many parts of England agricultural labourers threatened rebellion if they were too often given salmon to eat.

But when it comes to fishing for salmon – I mean with rod and line – few fish can compare to the mighty salmon for sheer fighting power. Only the carp and the barbel can match the salmon for sheer strength and dogged resistance.

But in many ways the salmon though powerful can seem the dunce of the fish class; when the water is just right and the fish are in the mood, they will throw themselves at the angler's bait one after another. The carp by contrast is a very suspicious customer who is not so easily fooled.

Much of the difficulty of catching salmon lies not in outwitting a cunning adversary, but in being at the river at the right time and having the skill to play a fish that, once hooked, behaves more like an express train than a living creature.

Extraordinary tales are often told of battles with giant salmon – this is a fish, let us not forget, that can reach weights of fifty pounds and more – but one of the most extraordinary salmon fishing stories I have ever heard was told to me by a gillie on the Spey.

Let us call him Old Jock. He loved to talk and more than that he loved a wee dram. The gift of a bottle of good whisky would always be repaid by Old Jock insisting that his gift-bearing friend must fish the best pools first.

Old Jock's favourite story was always delivered in a twinkling, incredulous style: 'I was out gillying for a gentleman from London. Very aristocratic but a good fisherman for all that. It should have been a great day – everything was right but your man could not rise a fish. Other anglers up and down the river were catching fish but it was as if my man had the plague and the fish knew it, but I wanted my tip at the end of the day and he was a generous man, but not a man who would be quite so generous if he failed to catch a fish.

'We tried everything. We changed flies. We flogged that water unmercifully and then in a moment my fisherman went from being the unluckiest man on the river to the luckiest and it was all through an incident that I have never heard happening anywhere else.

'He at last hooked a good fish which bored deep and then sulked in the deeper water, barely moving and unmovable for perhaps fifteen minutes or more. Then slowly that salmon began to tire. He looked to be about fifteen pounds when we at last spotted his ghostly form beneath the water. But what was this? Alongside our torpedo-like fish was another fish apparently identical to the hooked fish and each time our fish turned or made a rush one way or another his ghostly twin followed alongside.

'I got the net ready thinking that as our fish neared the shore his twin would move away, but when the beaten fish was just a few feet out I could still see his shadowy twin. Now, in this particular pool the water under our feet where we planned to net the hooked fish was perhaps two feet deep so I had prepared the net by pushing it down into that two feet of water. When at last my fisherman drew his hooked fish above my sunken net I began to lift. There was a mass of swirling and a great boil in the water as I did so and all for a moment was obscured. Then I felt the weight of the fish and knew all was well.

'But here's the shocker. As I hauled the net and its occupant up the bank I looked and realised that I had netted, not the hooked fish, but the ghostly twin, the fish that had never been hooked. My fisherman was still playing the other fish and he did so long enough for me to deal with the first fish in the net and land the second.

'It was an astonishing thing and an event I never expect to see repeated in my lifetime and I have never heard another tale of such an event from anyone else anywhere.'

C. D. Marot, *The Fishing Gazette*, July 1927

A Gathering of Giant Pike

THE ROADS were flooded, the verges drowned; lakes had spread wide across the fields. All along the valley of the lovely river Kennet water, water everywhere. In places the course of the river was completely lost. The normally narrow, twisting river looked more like the Thames where it meets the sea – a mile wide, featureless, the water dirty brown, the sky above iron grey.

What on earth was I doing planning a morning's fishing on such a river and on such a day?

Somehow, I had fooled myself into thinking that the old weir pool at Thatcham had enough in the way of steep banks to cope with this flood and keep within its banks. That might have been the case, but flooded fields meant I couldn't get to the weir pool anyway. What to do?

I tried half a mile downstream and managed – just – to get to the water's edge in a place where it might just be possible to cast a line. Having come this far I was determined at the very least to wet a line even if I would have to retreat defeated an hour later.

I had fished here before and remembered that 100 yards along the bank there was a side ditch that was normally filled with just a foot or two of water. On this day of flood, I found my ditch six feet deep in brown water but unlike the main river it was not flowing past me at thirty miles an hour.

Here, I thought, there might just be a big old chub or two resting out of the main current and picking off an occasional morsel that drifted in on the current. 'When it rains young man, there is only one bait. Your humble garden worm, and the bigger the better.' I had paid attention to that advice given to me so many years earlier and had a good bucket of worms on this day of biblical flooding.

I threw half a dozen of the biggest worms straight into the ditch, set up my rod with an old but well-oiled centrepin reel (no reel is better when a big fish makes that wild ferocious first run) and a peacock quill float.

I cast out and prepared to watch and wait for an hour or so before giving up and heading for home. I had absolutely no expectation of a bite let alone a fish.

Then happened one of those things that no angler has a right to expect. The float moved slowly across the ditch but hardly dipping at all. I had a size twelve hook on a cast of four-pound strength. 'This must be a chub,' I thought. 'Or maybe an eel. But whatever it is I will sing its praises just for livening up the day even if nothing else happens.'

I waited two or three seconds more and then lifted the rod smartly, expecting to have hooked a branch or other piece of submerged rubbish. Instead, there was heavy thump, thump, and something very determined moved off into the main river.

I leant into whatever it was to the point where I knew my line might break. The fish, if fish it was, held its position just ten feet or so out from the bank and remained quite still. I could hear the wind singing through my taut line. Stalemate. Five minutes passed and then the line came back onto the reel easily, my float reappeared out of the deep water and ... the

biggest pike I had ever seen in my life wallowed lazily on the surface.

It had hardly been a normal pike battle – by rights my four-pound line should have snapped like cotton with a pike of that size. It was a fish that should have rocketed across and down the river with me unable to stop it. Why was it so slow and sluggish?

I drew the monster over my landing net and needed two hands and all my strength to pull net and fish from the water. It was magnificent, tipping the scales at twenty-three pounds. It was a female and absolutely bursting with eggs and ready to spawn. It was semi-torpid and had picked up my worm probably out of sheer boredom, but had also been in no real mood to fight. Even so a twenty-three-pound pike caught on four-pound line and a worm was quite remarkable and from a relatively small river like the Kennet.

But more was to follow. I carefully returned the big fish to the water and cast again into the ditch. A few moments later exactly the same thing happened and I hooked another massive pike. Once again, against all the odds I hooked the fish at the edge of the mouth where its razor-sharp teeth could not cut the line. Once again, the fish simply used its great weight to reach the main river before slowly coming to the net. This one weighed eighteen pounds and was gravid like the first.

I returned it and fished on. No sooner had I started than another pike took the bait – this time a twenty-pounder which I also returned.

I had accidentally stumbled on a shoal of colossal female pike and I have no doubt I could have stayed and caught a dozen more, one after another and each almost the fish of a lifetime. How extraordinary I thought as I headed home that a day that should have been a washout, a blank, had turned into one of the most interesting days of my angling career.

A. J. Cross, *Angling*, 1906

Mixed Bag to Beat ...

HOW'S THIS for a day to remember? We were fishing an obscure Somerset river and between us in two hours we caught eels, tench, a bream or two, some rudd, plenty of lovely roach, a few dace, chub and gudgeon and then to top it all a flounder – a sea fish by heavens! – and a trout. Beat that if you can!

Hamilton Roberts, *The Sportsman*, 1870

Chapter 2

AGAINST THE ODDS

Barbel Landed on a Single Horsehair

FISHING FOR barbel with fine tackle is certainly productive of the most sport, though it is not the way to make a large bag; for, if the angler be using fine roach tackle and hooks a good fish, he may waste an hour and a half over him, and then lose him after all, as I have done scores of times.

I always fished with a single horsehair line formerly, when float fishing from a punt, and have landed very many barbel of four- and five-pounds weight with it; but so much time and so many fish were lost at it that I have long discontinued it.

I once remember, many years since, hooking an apparently large fish on a single hair, about five o'clock one November afternoon. I played him for a long time until my arm grew tired, when I handed the rod to a friend who was with me. He tired and gave the rod to Wisdom, who in turn, gave it back to me.

They both despaired of ever landing the fish and set his weight at a dozen pounds at least. 'He'll take you all night, sir,' said Wisdom.

'Then I'll stop with him all night if he does not break me, for I never have been able to land one of these big ones with a single hair,' was my reply.

I had often on the same spot hooked three or four of these monsters in a morning, but I never could land one of them. They always got away, for not far below us was a large deep hole, full of snags, old roots, and rubbish, and sooner or later they always remembered their hole there, and dashed into it headlong.

Even stout ledger tackle would hardly have held them and that they were very shy at, preferring the single hair greatly. This hole was about fifty yards below us, and I constantly expected the fish would make for it. However, though he made constant runs, he never cared to go above half the distance, but sheered about, now out in the stream, and now in towards the bank.

It had long been dark, and he showed no symptoms of tiring, though he had in turn tired all of us. Playing a fish in the dark is awkward work, so we hailed some men, several of whom, attracted by the report of our having hooked a big un', were standing on the bank, to bring us a couple of lanthorns and some hot brandy and water for it was bitterly cold; and with the aid of the lanthorns we at length managed to get the net under the fish and lifted him out. It was half past eight when he was landed, so that I had him on three and a half hours. And now what does the reader think he weighed?

I was disgusted to find that he was only a six-and-a-half-pound fish; had I known it I would have broken from him hours before; but it turned out that he was hooked by the back fin, and his head being perfectly free, he of course played as

heavily as a fish of double the size; and even now, remembering what the stream was, I wonder how I did succeed in landing him, as a fish so hooked, having his broadside opposed to the water, has great powers of resistance.

Indeed, I consider that the accomplishment was equal to landing a fish of double the weight if properly hooked.

The feat may sound incredible – three and a half hours with only a single horsehair, a fin-hooked fish, and a heavy stream – nevertheless it is strictly true. Had the hold been in the mouth instead of the hard tough fin, it would probably have cut out half the time.

Francis Francis, *A Book on Angling*, 1896

Beginner's Luck and a Novice Sea Trout

MY FIRST introduction to fly fishing was with the sea trout, and it came about in this way: forty-two years ago, strolling down Princes Street, Edinburgh, I came to a shop in which the goods were being sold by auction. The lot then selling was 'a beautiful fly rod, reel, book of flies, line, and basket, all going for ten shillings'. I bid sixpence more and the lot was mine, and I became the happy possessor of what to me at that time was a white elephant.

I had never fished. The lot was deposited in a cupboard. I will not say what I thought of myself in cooler moments for having thrown away what was then to me a considerable sum. However, some few weeks after, strolling along the banks of the Eden in Fifeshire, I came upon a fisherman, and after watching him casting his fly and killing some fine sea trout, the thought struck me: why not try and do the same with the lot in the cupboard; it appears very easy. So that evening the fishing paraphernalia were rummaged out, and the next morning I made an early start for the river. No one there to give me a hint what to do; but the rod was put together, the line run through the rings, the reel adjusted, the casting line clumsily attached, and a fly selected from the book, I well recollect, a green body and grey wings, and I tried to cast the line into the stream.

Well, never shall I forget that first cast. Not having secured the top joint, that and the line shot well into the river. And again I soon found the fly entangled in the line; that was got clear; then when casting again I found no fly at the end of the line! Another was put on: a peculiar kind of crack behind me when casting and lo this fly was gone. What was to be done? Try another fly: no better result.

First it hit a stone, then the line got tangled into strange knots that took half an hour to unravel; patience was getting exhausted – the whole lot shall go to the first boy I meet – the art of fly fishing was too much for me. Another cast, however, to see whether I could not be more successful. To my surprise the fly went out straight into the ripple, there was a break of the water, and the line tightened. Fortunately, the reel was free. Away went the line, the rod bent – I had hooked a fish, and after most gentle and patient working, I landed a beautiful silvery sea trout of a pound and a half. How I managed it I cannot tell, but I drew him gently out to a flat bit of sand, threw the rod down, and rushed at my prey, and with both hands cast him far away from the water. This gave me courage. With a short line I found I could get the fly on the water, and in about an hour or so had managed to land three fish without losing another fly. I came home in triumph, and prided myself on knowing how to throw a fly, but was soon disabused of this bit of conceit. The next day dire misfortune awaited me: flies were whipped off, the line got twisted, a large fish broke me in the first rush.

I was in despair, when, as fortune would have it, I met the fisherman I had seen the first day, entered into conversation with him, and related my mishaps. At once he gave me every encouragement, pointed out faults, made me fish and throw the fly whilst he gave directions, and with the utmost patience gave me some most valuable hints, and from that time I looked upon fly fishing as a sport not to be despised, and no one could become a more enthusiastic lover of the rod and line.

Edward Hamilton, Fly Fishing, 1884

A Whopper in the Weir

ONE DAY in April, some years ago, before the Thames was disfigured and bereft of half its beauties by the hideous iron erections with which the conservators had thought proper to replace the picturesque old weirs, a young man might have been seen industriously holding his rod over one of the lashers near Marsh Lock, while the fierce rush of water beneath him kept the bait spinning rapidly, and more often out of the water than in it.

He aspired to catch a Thames trout, but had hitherto not been successful. In those comparatively halcyon days, before the great invasion of the Thames by the steam water-carriages more particularly beloved of the snobocracy and bean-feasters, there was some pleasure in fishing for trout from the weir. Old water-stained and moss-grown camp-sheathing, kept up by ancient piles, surrounded the swirling pool, and supported a bank on which grew the great burdock, blue forget-me-nots, meadowsweet, and the other wild flowers and weeds which lovers of the Thames know so well.

Two foaming, boiling, frothing streams leapt into the great pool, and it was in one of these that our friend believed that sooner or later a trout would take his bait.

But the fish ignored his silvery bleak, and towards evening an old doctor – a noted fisherman in his day – strolled on to the weir and asked, with a twinkle in his eye, the question, 'What sport?'

The youth replied, with truth, 'Not much,' adding thereto the superfluous words 'at present.'

The doctor looked up and the doctor looked down, and close to an overhanging bush he noticed half a dozen minnows leap out of the water. 'You have a splendid rod,' he said; 'would you allow me to try it?'

'It ought to be good,' drawled the youth; 'it cost a heap of money.'

'And perhaps you would allow me to take a cast with it?' said the old angler.

The youth had no objection, but rather thought casting a mistake.

The doctor readjusted the bait, drew some line off the reel – Nottingham reels were unknown on the Thames in those days – and with great care and precision sent the bleak through the air, and let it fall, with the smallest possible splash, close to the overhanging bush. Then he commenced to draw the line in rapidly, and before two coils had fallen on the grass there was a sudden check, the rod bent, and a lovely trout of some five pounds leapt into the air. There followed a gallant fight. Right across the weir pool dashed the trout, as gamely as any salmon, and charged into the lasher, making a brave but futile attempt to get into the upper reach of the river. But no beginner was handling the rod. Erect and calm the old man stood, keeping the point of the rod well up, bearing heavily on the fish when he approached a dangerous place, but dealing with him tenderly when in open water. At the end of some ten or twelve minutes the trout turned over on his side, and was brought close to the side.

But the net was a small one, and the youth bungled. Fortunately, the fish was well hooked.

'Hold the rod, sir,' said the doctor; 'hold the rod!'

The youth obeyed, and the more experienced of the two took the net, and in a moment the fish was landed.

At this point angling stories of great success generally leave off, but to this one there is a short epilogue.

'Have you got anything to put the fish in?' queried the doctor.

'Oh, yes,' said the other; 'I have a basket.'

'That's right; but you had better empty the things out of it.'

The youth obeyed, lined the basket with grass, and in it laid the fish.

'It's really very good of you to lend me your creel,' said the doctor; 'the trout is just what I wanted for a patient of mine!' and before the youth could find words to express what he very much wanted to say, the doctor had left the weir, taking trout and basket with him.

The feelings of that junior angler can, perhaps, be better imagined than described. For fully half an hour he sat and pondered; but then, having got into a thoroughly philosophical frame of mind, went home and told his friends how he had caught his first Thames trout, how Doctor K had kindly assisted in landing it, and how he had generously presented the trout to the doctor for a sick friend.

John Bickerdyke, *Days of My Life*, 1895

Thames Miracle

NO ONE had heard of trout being caught from the Lower Thames in more than a century. In the 1960s the river was still little more than an open sewer downstream of Putney, but despite the chemicals and dirt, the rubbish, old bikes and supermarket trollies littering the foreshore, a few hardy anglers still set off for the river on days when the tide was right and rainfall had livened up the grey soupy river.

The giant roach that inhabited the broad reaches of the river at Isleworth, Kew and Chiswick were one of the few species that could survive the low oxygen levels caused by the pollution. Indeed, the roach thrived and grew big precisely because there was so little competition from species less well adapted to the poor water quality.

Roach weighing more than two pounds were almost common at one time but they were caught only by those who knew the river intimately. Three-pounders were by no means rare and anyone who has tried to catch a really big roach will know just how remarkable a fish of that size really is.

My Uncle Jack came from a long line of Thames fishers. His grandfather owned his own punt at Richmond and knew the tricky art of setting the punt so it would rise and fall on its poles as the river rose and fell.

'Very easy to get into trouble if you don't know what you're doing,' he used to say to anyone who showed any inclination to join him on a Sunday morning. 'If the punt sticks on one of its poles you'll be tipped in and the river runs fast and deep – it might rise ten or twelve feet as it comes up.'

Uncle Jack had caught many big fish from his grandfather's punt; bream to eight pounds, dace to over a pound and he'd caught two roach over the magical three-pound mark.

But Uncle Jack's favourite story had nothing to do with roach or bream. He had decided early one summer morning not to fish from the punt, but instead he wandered down to Chiswick where in the 1960s Old Church Street still had a few beautiful eighteenth-century houses – the remnants of dozens of such houses, all destroyed because of our obsession with the motor car, or as Jack used to put it, 'the bloody infernal combustion engine'. He hated cars and had never learned to drive, relying instead on an old bicycle to carry him up and down the Thames. The fact that his lack of transport limited him to the lower Thames never upset him.

'No one knows the river as well as I do,' he would say, 'because I never fish anywhere else.'

On reaching the river at the end of Church Street he wandered down the old slipway and waded straight into the river in his old black gumboots. He always fished with either bread, cheese or worms as bait and on this day for reasons he was never able to explain he chose a large garden worm.

'I wanted to see what might be there so I used a whopping great worm,' he said. 'Must have been six or eight inches long. Like a bloomin' eel!'

He cast out and waited. The worm sat on its hook about a foot from a small lead weight. Jack was a great believer in simple tackle. He felt it bump along the bottom and began to daydream, admiring the view down to Hammersmith Bridge, cursing the rowers and idle passers-by who insisted on shouting, ' 'Ad any luck, mate?' at him.

A minute or two more passed and then something extraordinary happened.

'I could almost feel the worm and the weight trickling across the gravel as the current tumbled it downstream,' said Jack. 'Then without warning there was a bang; no little tentative plucks as you might get from a roach or bream, there was a bang. At the time I thought it must be an audible bang so violent did it seem. After the bang the line began to be torn off the reel. It all happened so quickly that the friction from the speeding line burned my finger. When I came to my senses half the line had gone from the reel and the rod top was bucking violently, but at least the beast, whatever it was had stopped its run. I kept the point of the rod up while the fish chugged first upstream and then down but always out in the middle of the river. I was baffled. That first run had felt like a salmon, a carp or a barbel. This fish might just have been a carp though at this time no carp had been caught this low down in the river and a salmon was impossible to imagine, a barbel nearly impossible. As I pondered all this the fish made another high-speed dash and I could feel it kiting across the current, using the pressure of the moving water on its flank to put more pressure on the rod. I was convinced he would escape or a stupid rowing boat would row over my line and cut through it. But the gods were with me and ten minutes later a tired fish wallowed twenty feet in front of me – it was a big brown trout. In perfect condition. It was clearly a wild fish rather than a stocked fish – who would stock the Thames at Chiswick with trout? – and for a river that had not been known to harbour trout for a century and more it was big – perhaps three pounds. Three pounds is a good trout but this fish had fought like a ten-pounder. The explanation was not far to seek – when I got that big old trout in the net, I could see quite clearly that I had hooked it in the tail. A three-pound fish of any species hooked in the tail always fights like a fish three times its size and it will usually throw the hook so I was uniquely lucky in two respects – I'd caught that rarest of fish a Thames trout and despite hooking it in the tail I'd landed it. This really was the fish of a lifetime because it was the last fish, except perhaps a salmon, anyone would have expected from this part of the river.'

Jack carefully unhooked his trout and placed it gently back in the river where, with luck, it is still swimming today.

Tim Kehoe, *Angling*, 1951

Salmon on Horsehair and Hazel

WE ONCE saw a shepherd boy, in Peebleshire, land a prime salmon, of twelve-pounds weight, with a common hazel rod, and an extraordinary hair line, without a reel or winch of any kind upon it, and with a fly exactly like a large humble bee. He hooked the fish in the deep part of a strong stream, and had the sagacity and promptitude of action to throw his rod immediately into the water after the rushing and powerful fish. The force of the current took it down to the calmer end of the stream, where the stripling caught hold of it again, and instantly succeeded in running the salmon into the next stream, and so on till he had artfully exhausted his captive, and forced him into a shallow part of the water. Here he got him stranded with great adroitness, and eventually conquered him in capital style.

Robert Blakey, Angling, 1840

Nothing Goes Right and Then Nothing Goes Wrong

BUT, TO our humble business. The swell of the river had been trifling, and it would be fit to fish on the morrow. The later in the day, said Walter the Bold, the better; so, I fidgeted away the early part of the morning, and hauled over my

London tackle, which proved unseemly to the sight of the Scotchman.

The flies, he said, were dressed like dancing dogs; but my rod, he owned, was fine.

At last, we started. We had about two or three miles to go to the upper cast, called the Carry-wheel. As I neared it, and saw the sweep of the gallant river, I stepped out in eagerness till I came to the top of a steep covered with wood, gorse, and broom; then I dashed down the rocks, and found myself on the channel, with the rush of a glorious salmon cast before me.

Think of this, ye gudgeon fishers!

The rod was put together in haste – out came the London book of flies; and while I selected that misnomer, a metropolitan salmon fly, a huge fish sprang out of the water before me, bright and lusty.

What a challenge! In my agitation the flies got entangled; confusion worse confounded beset me.

The hooks stuck into my quivering fingers, and then a puff of wind scattered the flies abroad in various directions. To crown all, Walter kept me in a perspiration by making, as if he would throw for the fish, which, by anticipation, I considered as my property. At length I collected my senses, and my flies also; and it is a wonder that I did so, as the said fish continued his gambols, and repeatedly claimed my attention.

Now then for it. The cast being narrow at the throat, I began with a short line, which I kept lengthening as it got wider; for so it became me.

I came now, step by step, to the spot where I expected to do for the fish. Excited as I was, I flung with spirit; but the fly alighted not upon the wave; far from it; it attached itself most perfectly to a birch tree in my rear, and crack went my top-varnished Higginbotham rod.

Thus I was at once discomfited almost in the arms of victory. Being totally driven from my propriety, I cannot be answerable for what I said or did: something very sublime

it was, no doubt; but let that pass. Certain it was that each particular hair of my head stood on end with horror. As I had spare tops to my rod, I soon set all to rights again. But throw, and throw as I would, the salmon would not come and be caught; so I gave up the unreasonable brute at last as unattainable. Nor could my Scottish companion make any hand of him afterwards. In fishermen's language, I had set him down.

The tail of the cast now grew broader, and it was necessary to wade; so, in I went, accoutred as I was; that is to say, in light, flimsy walking shoes, without nails. I soon perceived that the wet stones were slippery and treacherous beyond endurance, and that my shoes had no adhesive qualities. My untutored feet took no hold, and I floundered about in the superlative degree, quite innocent of a due balance. At length, joyous to relate, I saw a break in the water, and the switch of a fish's tail: I struck, and found I had him fast. As for playing him, I did no such thing; on the contrary, I honestly confess that he played me, and had all along the best of it too – for I could not keep my footing. I swayed like a pendulum, only more unevenly, till down I went from a treacherous stone, which joggled under my step, and tilted me in about middle deep. Being thus sufficiently humid, I beat a retreat as soon as I was able, and backed out on the channel: arrived there, I felt the beauty of my new situation, and made certain of a capture. The monster was still strong, and sprang out of the water, as if to show me what a prize I was about to obtain, and I acknowledged his value secretly. He next judged it prudent to give a sudden turn, a sort of ill-natured twist – an obstinate obliquity of motion that I shall never forget, or forgive: at once my muscles ceased to quiver – the line lost its strain and sprang aloft in thin air, and the rod was as straight as when it came from the maker's hands. Here was an exposition! here was a horror! To crown all, Walter stood by and took snuff most provokingly philosophical, and I thought I detected a half-suppressed smile on his visage. Raving as I was internally, I still conducted myself with outward decency, particularly when I found that the fish was lost owing to the bad temper of a London hook, which broke during the battle; so that I, Harry Otter, was not to blame after all. I gave one solemn sigh for the death of old Kirby, whose hooks would not have broken in the mouth of a shark.

My Scottish friend now fitted me out with one of his own flies, but desired me not to throw any more in the Carrywheel; 'For,' said he, 'as sure as deid, the spirit is against ye: he hampered yer heucks, he broke yer goad and yer flee, and he pulled ye doon in the waters; and ye never would hae been seen again in this life, gin I hadna cotched ye by the oxter. Thae that the Kelpie grips seldom rise again; but nae ither spirit, ye ken, has power in the rinnin water.'

Whether one believes in superstition or not matter not, but I left the cast because it was unlucky, which is much the same thing.

I was now under the influence of some better spirit of the flood; for I absolutely landed two grilse of six pounds each in a cast called The Noirs. Wattie, seeing my rod bent, came up: he said but little; but that little was the most unqualified abuse of my mismanagement. The fact is, I treated the grilse just as I would have treated a trout; a very base mistake. I bagged them, however, notwithstanding – thanks to the excellence of the channel.

The next cast I came to was called The Brig-end; and here I hooked a fine salmon: he was brave and strenuous, and so ponderous, that it seemed as if my hook had caught hold of a floating Norwegian pine, 'fit for the mast of some high admiral'. After various eccentric courses, Master Fish made a sudden and desperate rush down the river; out went my line with a whirring rattle, and cut one of my fingers sharply. I followed as best I might, prancing in the water like a war horse, with the spray about my ears. Wattie hallooed out, and

said I know not what; but the tone of his voice was far from being complimentary. Nearly all my line of a hundred yards was now run out; when the fish made a sudden turn, crossed to the opposite bank, and coasted up it amongst the rocks. Here again Wattie was perfectly wild.

'Gang back, I tell ye, haud up yer gaud, shorten yer line – keep aboon him, ye gomrell! Ou, ye are arownit assure as deeth! Pin in, pin in – pin out, pin out!'

These contradictory exclamations I could have excused, as I believe they were warranted by the sudden turns of the fish; but the fellow had absolutely the temerity to attempt to take my rod from me, whereat I lashed out behind, and gave him sundry kicks, as strong and hearty as could be managed with my degenerate shoes.

I did shorten my line a little, however; but the water pressed against it so heavily that I could not extricate it as I wished. I had now receded to the shore, and gained, as I thought, the victory. Being resolved to be canny, I fixed my eyes intently upon the point where the line dipped into the water, under which I conceived the fish to be; but to my surprise I caught a glimpse of my playfellow with the tail of my eye, springing out of the water, and towing my tackle after him about twenty yards above the spot where I conceived him to be. I was in a perfect tremor – ye gods, how I did shake! But that did not last long, as the line all of a sudden vaulted into the air, and streamed abroad like the lithe pennon on a ship-mast, being, at a rude guess, about twenty yards minus of its pristine proportions.

This was all magic to me at the time – magic of the most distressing sort; but in after days, I saw what my error

was. I knew that it consisted in giving out too much line at first, which would have been unnecessary, had I stepped back at once on the channel, kept my rod aloft, and ran down the riverside with my fish, still keeping above him. This, as has been seen, I did not do; but kept deep in the water, where I could make but little way. With a shorter line, and good footing, I might have kept above my fish when he crossed over and made up the stream, and thus have held the line tight; but as it was, it hung back in a huge sweep, that would have gone round the foundations of another Carthage – which sweep, coming in contact with a concealed rock or stone, gave the fish a dead pull, and he broke it incontinently.

It was very distressing – very.

Now having your line in this untoward position is called being drowned, and the breaking of the tackle in the manner described being cut – soul-harrowing, suicidal miseries, that no one can properly describe.

Here ended my fishing, and in summing up the events of the day I had not much to congratulate myself upon. I had been guilty of almost every error possible: I broke my hook and my rod; I was moreover cut and drowned, technically speaking. I learned, however, four things: firstly, never to fish in a cast where the Kelpie has his stronghold; secondly, to look occasionally behind me before my throw, where the banks are steep and near; thirdly, to try the strength of my hook before I use it, not after; and, fourthly, to get into shoes of a proper consistency, and well studded with nails of Brobdingnag dimensions. Take warning, gentle readers, from these disasters, which are recounted for your benefit and instruction.

But bear this in mind also; the day following, my fortunes were utterly transformed and from a day when nothing went right, I found myself in a place and time where nothing could go wrong; for I landed seven salmon in one short evening.

William Scrope, Days and Nights of
Salmon Fishing in the Tweed, 1854

The Last of the Thames Trout

BY THE time we had reached the early 1980s no one really believed that the lower Thames would ever again provide a home for the big wild brown trout for which it had once been famous. Not only that but even small trout were no longer ever caught or seen. The growth in towns and villages and riverside houses and all the pollution that accompanies them had made the river too dirty for a fish that needs bright highly oxygenated water.

True the Thames was far cleaner in London than it had been for more than a century and a half, but the gradual decline of the Thames further out bothered no one except perhaps a few old fishermen who remembered that the weirs at Shepperton and even Teddington had once contained big trout. The decline of the river as a trout fishery was seen as just a sad but unavoidable consequence of house, road and factory building and of course house, road and factory building must always come first. We might save an odd tiny corner for nature to appease our consciences but the wealthy and the property developers cared nothing for the river and those among them who enjoyed fishing for trout merely headed for the wilds of Scotland or Wales, places not yet unduly damaged by property development.

A few wild optimists of course still convinced themselves that trout might survive in the middle river, perhaps where the stream still ran fast below well oxygenated weir water, but others laughed at them.

I too was once of the sceptical mockers – until one extraordinary day on the Thames at Windsor.

I was spinning for pike one autumn on the home park, that part of the royal estate at Windsor where the Windsor

Horse Show had been held for a century or more and a part of the park therefore to which the public were admitted.

I had fished below the railway bridge that crosses the river here and had landed several good pike. Today the river was running faster than usual after a few days of rain. The spinner landed halfway across the river and I felt it swinging round in the current as I reeled it back in towards me. Time after time I cast in the same manner taking a few steps downstream between each cast, just as one would when fishing for salmon. Nothing. It felt hopeless, but I decided I would try one last cast and then head for home.

The spinner came round as usual thrumming gently at the end of the line. Then there were two almighty thumps at the end of the line and something heavy and powerful began boring deep and away from me down the fast-flowing water and heading for the far side of the river.

Despite my ten-pound line and powerful pike rod the fish it seemed was quite unstoppable. Line poured from the reel; I leaned dangerously into the fish convinced the hook would slip or the line break. With just a few turns of the line left on the reel, the fish stopped and lay absolutely doggo for the next ten minutes.

Suddenly it kited across the river to my side but at least 100 yards downstream.

Time passed and little by little I regained line. Two more heart-stopping rushes took place with all my line disappearing before the fish decided to head upstream and back towards me at speed. It stopped mid-river and perhaps thirty feet out directly in front of me.

I was convinced it was a twenty-pound pike at least or a ten-pound chub.

Slowly, slowly the fish rose and came towards me. I got the net ready. When I saw what finally breached the surface I almost fell in, such was my astonishment. There at the end of the line was a beautiful brown trout, golden buttery in colour with huge glowing spots.

In my moment of elation and bafflement I fumbled the net and really should have lost that trout but the gods were with me, or perhaps lady luck; either way that wonderful fish slid into the net.

Then the real surprise. The trout though perfect in every way, weighed just two pounds eight ounces so why had it fought so long and hard? The answer was that it was hooked neatly through the top of its tail fin.

The hooks should certainly have fallen out long before I had any idea what was on the end of my line, but for some extraordinary reason they did not. Ninety-nine times out of a hundred in these circumstances such a fish would have escaped and become a tale of the giant that got away. This instead was truly the tale of the one that didn't get away! In fifty years of fishing the Thames it was my one and only trout and I knew as I slipped it back into the water that I would never catch another.

Martin Fagan, *Angling*, 1981

A Hopeless Chance ...

THE ONE great ingredient in successful fly fishing, as in most other fishing, is patience. The man whose fly is always on the water has the best chance.

I am a great sticker myself, and never like to give it up.

There is always a chance of a fish or two, no matter how hopeless it looks.

You never know what may happen in fly fishing.

I have, scores and scores of times, seen a bit of luck at the last moment, which turned a bad day into a good one.

The very last day that I fished last season was one of the best instances of this that has happened to me for a long time.

There had been rain, and the water was coloured, and it was a cold blusterous day. A few small fish rose under the banks, of which I got a brace about half a pound each.

Evening came on; I went to the most likely part of the stream – a corner below a mill; there I found the best rod in our club, who hadn't a fish.

He had fished all the best places carefully, and had done nothing.

It was getting towards dark, and he left for home. I walked with him for a chat for about half a mile, when I returned to the mill, my way lying in a different direction. When I left my friend, I took down my cast and reeled up the line, though the rod was still together. I had a companion with me, who urged me to have another cast below the mill, as he knew there were some good fish there.

It was the most hopeless chance to look at I ever saw – almost dark, bitterly cold and blusterous. I would have bet fifty to one against even a rise. I put up the line again and rose a fish at the first cast, and hooked him at the second.

I hooked three fish at that corner in about twenty minutes, two of which were about one and a half pounds each, and the other three pounds, besides rising and scratching two or three more.

It was marvellous.

Francis Francis, *Angling*, 1883

Right up to the Wire

A VERY keen and expert dry fly fisherman, the late Mr Harry Maxwell, one of the best of friends and anglers, once showed me a method of taking fish lying with their tails against a wire fencing that crossed the Test at right angles, the wire moreover being barbed. I was fishing in Hurstbourne Park, and he was accompanying me, as he often did, with his field-glass. Below the 'cascade' a four- or five-stranded barbed wire fence went straight across the water. Just above it, in midstream, in the stickle, a plump, transparent-looking Test fish of about one and a half pounds had taken up his position, and was boldly taking every fly within reach. My friend told me to catch him, and I said at once I did not know how to do it without getting hung up. He then explained his dodge, which may be carried out as follows.

Having waded in below the fish, take some loose coils of line off the reel in the left hand, then cast well above, and let the dry well-cocked fly float down to him. If he accepts it and comes down under the fence slack off the loose coils, get up to the fence as quickly as possible, pass the rod under and over, and then you are free to play the trout below you. If, on the other hand, he refuses the fly, do not attempt to recover the line in the usual manner or you will inevitably be hung up. Simply lower your rod point to the water, and then the quiet drag of the stream will bring your cast and fly slowly up and over the fence, even although the fly had floated a foot or two downstream and under the wire. The action is so slow and even that there is no chance of being entangled in the wires, and as a fish in such a position thinks he is in possession of a vantage-point, and is seldom fished for, he is generally a bold feeder.

Having explained the method, my friend made me try the cast myself, and the first fly floating near enough to tempt the fish was taken boldly; the whole manoeuvre succeeded, and I was able to land my trout below me.

H. V. Hart-Davis,
Chats on Angling, 1906

The Duck-Eating Golden Pike

THE PURSUIT of rabbits being incomplete, M returned to his former occupation, but S fished again, continually finding sport of the miscellaneous kind, such as a chub with cheese paste, perch with dew worm out of the milk-prepared moss, roach rod with running tackle, and leger tackle on a spinning rod. With this and a great worm on a strong hook he had the surprise of a fight that gave him not a little concern. The fish at first appeared to be going to ground, even boring bodily into it. Then it gave way to panic, and shot about the pool as if pursued by a water fiend. Winched in slowly, it plunged into the bank, thought better of it, and ran up stream. At this crisis M arrived, commandeered the net, and stood around offering advice. It was a monster eel, he said. Lean into him; be careful; be more energetic; certainly, all right.

The last remark was simply a receipt in form of a little speech from S, who had briefly bidden him to mind his own business. The unseen fish abruptly had given in. Was it collapse? Slowly, slowly it followed the revolution of the reel, both men peering intent for first sight and grounds for identification of species. The first sight, however, must have been on the part of the fish, which went off in a fright deep down with renewed strength, and then it did surrender, a

barbel of six pounds, a somewhat rare fish for the river, and only taken when, as in this case, it had wandered up into the weir pool.

Having told M to mind his own business with a minimum of ceremony, it was not surprising that S was left alone, not exactly to his sport, since, as it happened, the barbel closed his account, unless one or two losses may be included in that definition, and, to give him his due, he was so thorough a fisherman that he did regard losses, shortcomings, and mishaps as legitimate assets in the general game. He had forgotten in his barbel absorption to enquire, according to usage, how his comrade had been faring, and did not meet him again till they were in the throat of the lane cottage-wards bound.

'Well, old 'un; what luck with the paternoster?' he asked, cheerily. M, with a sly twinkle in the eye, said, yes, he had done somewhat; three pike. It may be premised that the young men had both been trying at intervals for a certain marauding pike reported to them as a ferocious duck destroyer by a gentleman farmer who came down to gossip. He indicated the field and a gravel pit as a guide to the place where his cowman had seen a duckling seized by a pike, and the man embellished his account by swearing that the fish had ploughed his way down the river half out of water, with the ball of feathers bewhiskering his jaws. Manford, it seems, had revenged the raided ducks. A large pike lay at the bottom of his rush basket underneath three jack and a covering of rushes, and it was produced as a crowning show, a golden fish of seventeen pounds lured to the bank by a small spinner. There was talk of nothing else that night but this prize at the keeper's cottage, village taproom, at the lock-heads, and by five-barred gates; and the exultant keeper, who took credit for all, was heard to say that it was the best bloomin' jack he had seen 'for seven year come last plum blight,' whenever and whatever that might be.

William Senior, *Lines in Pleasant Places*, 1920

Three Wild Days in Wessex

IT WAS hard to understand at the time why, at the natural and innocent enquiry as to his favourite bait, the local expert should suddenly shut up like some sensitive plant.

He had been nobly and generously expansive, measuring his catches of fish as if they were coals, by the sack, but now he was reticent and cautious. 'Sometimes I use one thing, sometimes another,' he said.

The reason for the change of attitude became clear later (when he was one day discovered in close proximity to a net), but for the present it mattered not.

It was enough that he had revealed where fishing was to be had which, if you were planning to take the fish home with you, required the substitution, he insisted, of a sack instead the more ordinary and modest wicker creel, and there was no unnecessary delay in putting this important discovery to the proof. A sack, two sacks – for there were two anglers – were put into the waggonette with the tackle and lunch, and the river was reached before 10 a.m. had struck by the church clock on the hill.

It was not a promising day; summer, after two months of hopeless severity, appeared to be endeavouring to surpass itself, and leaden masses of cloud swept across the sky at the bidding of a rushing, mighty wind. But the river, seen from the high stone bridge on which we were standing, looked as attractive as the keenest seeker after free fishing could desire.

Above the bridge was a broad gravel shallow on which were doubtless the dace of which the local expert had spoken, and, it might be, a trout or so as well. In the distance the mill could be seen through some trees, and a point above the shallow where two streams met suggested a backwater as well as the millstream, and presumably a weir pool. Below

the bridge the river curved away among trees in a tempting succession of stream and pool.

The problem, inevitable on a new and unknown water, arose: what was to be fished for, and where? The fly seemed hopeless in such a wind, the shallows were no better than a storm-swept sea, and indeed, so far as could be seen, the water above the bridge was shelterless.

Below, a clump of trees a meadow's distance away offered more hope, and thither our expert companion strode firmly, without wasting words. His instinct proved to have been right; the river turned a sharp corner under the shadow of the trees, forming as perfect a pool for perch as could be met with. The rods were quickly put together, and soon two red worms were offering wriggling attractions to the fish in two convenient eddies, and the anglers sat somewhat sheltered from the icy blast.

Almost immediately our expert companion's float disappeared, and a fish was hooked, which turned out to be a nice perch of nearly a pound; it fought gamely, but the pool was too deep for weeds, and the net soon claimed its own, while the wind shrieked with renewed vigour, as though to celebrate the success. Our companion then set off to try his worm elsewhere on the river and for us who remained there began such an hour of sport as may never come again.

The fish seemed literally mad for the fly, and black gnat, soldier palmer, and coachman were all taken with instant impartiality; and it seemed that the dace were all big ones, running between half and three-quarters of a pound. Several times two were on the cast together, and once even three, of which one got off.

Many were lost; in such a wind it could not be otherwise, for it was impossible to attempt to humour a lightly hooked fish; but we estimated we must have caught twenty pounds total in weight of fish by lunchtime.

Our expert friend reappeared. He had, he complained, been prevented from making a phenomenal bag of perch by the trivial circumstance of a tree being blown down into the very pool which he was fishing.

As it was, he had only caught eleven, with three roach of a pound each, and, the tree having disturbed the river somewhat, he had also set out to explore. Exploration was, however, interrupted by the coming of the rain, which had so far held off, and the day's fishing ended prematurely. Nevertheless, as we went homewards we agreed that the local expert was a very estimable person, and that we were singularly fortunate in having stumbled on a piece of free fishing which even the English climate could not render bad. When the weather improved, we assured each other, we should do something remarkable in the history of angling; all that was necessary was a little patience until the gales should have blown themselves out. Summer cannot always disguise itself as winter, and after two months we were entitled to hope for better things.

So, we waited our chance and studied a depressed and unsympathetic barometer.

At last, one morning the wind dropped and my expert friend greeted me at breakfast with the words, 'It's going up!'

I hastened to verify this glad intelligence. Sure enough the needle on the barometer had moved; it no longer presaged seismic convulsions and disheartening phenomena of that kind, as it had been doing for some weeks, but was content to indicate 'rain'. This, my companion pointed out, clearly meant a fine day, since no barometer could be expected to recover itself all in a moment from such upheavals as we had been having, and any upward movement at all was a sign of complete change; now therefore was our expected opportunity. The greyness of the sky, he explained, was a sure sign of midday heat.

We started accordingly. During the drive I surveyed the heavens with suspicion, and when we reached the bridge,

I called his attention to a certain rumbling noise that was going on in the distance. I am always diffident about rumbling noises when I am out fishing; one has read horrible stories about fire falling from heaven upon the angler, by way of his rod, and consuming him. But the expert knows no panics of this kind; he said it was 'guns on Salisbury Plain'. Those weapons also, in some obscure way, seemed to account for the oppressiveness of the air and the indubitable masses of heavy cloud that hung low at all points of the compass. Having explained these things, he led the way upstream to the weir pool, which we had decided to fish that day. It was a deep, still hole, with very little current coming over the sill, and to me had a dark and dismal appearance; I never can take a cheerful view of any water when there is a rumbling noise in the distance. However, the rods were fitted together, some groundbait was thrown into the pool, and we began to fish for roach.

There were no bites, and apparently no fish in the pool to cause them. Presently, too, I felt called upon to observe that the guns on Salisbury Plain must be getting nearer, since the sound was steadily increasing in volume.

My friend suggested that a breeze was getting up and was assisting the noise to travel. But there was no breeze, and, so far as I could see, no excuse for his equanimity. Before long I was compelled to ask ironically if he thought there were guns all round us, because the rumbling was now plainly coming from several directions at once, and to the meanest intelligence was obvious and alarming thunder. He admitted rather regretfully that there did seem to be thunder about, and after an awe-inspiring clap remarked that there must be a good storm somewhere; when it broke the fish would wake up. He had long been curious to find out whether fish really did feed well in a thunderstorm. With this he threw in another handful of groundbait.

I, however, had risen when the last peal began. My interest in the scientific effect of electricity was languid. I said:

'There are three good storms, and in about three minutes they will be here. I don't believe the most perverted fish would bite in three thunderstorms, and I shan't wait to see.'

The indomitable one laughed, and I fled, taking refuge in the sitting room of a little farm hard by the mill. We neither of us know to this day whether fish will bite in three thunderstorms better than in one or none, because even the indomitable one was compelled to retreat before the torrential downpour that began in a few minutes and lasted until after five. The mill formed a convenient centre for three separate storms, each one more violent than the other, and we spent an unprofitable day looking out of the window and watching the lightning as it played about and destroyed the surrounding country. When the rain did stop eventually the river was the colour of pea soup, and roach fishing being out of the question, we went home disconsolate.

After this the barometer needle went back to its prognostication of earthquakes, and the indomitable one refused to fish any more. It was not that his heart quailed before our English summer, but that it was filled with righteous indignation. A refusal to fish seemed to him the only way in which he could mark his disapproval of the weather. I acknowledged that he was right, but still I badly wanted to try the stream again, for I was certain that its possibilities were untold. So, one morning I thought of the old adage which promises sunshine before eleven if it has been raining before seven. It was raining nicely at half past six, and a brisk wind got up about nine. There was just a chance when I started that this would dissipate the clouds and give the sun its opportunity. I took a fly rod and set out in my waders and a short mackintosh coat, determined to give the dace on the shallow another trial. The water was reached about half past ten, just when the clearing-up ought to have begun, if there was any truth in adages, which there is not. As a matter of fact, the rain chose that time to begin in real earnest, and continued vigorously for the rest of the day.

I endured many things, including sodden sandwiches for lunch, and persevered in spite of them all. But the fish did not seem to appreciate my efforts. It may be that Wessex dace demand more violent weather than was vouchsafed to them that day. The wind, it is true, was creditable, and the rain did its best, but there was no mad rise such as there had been before.

The fish came short, and it was not until I retired to the shelter of the bridge and added to each fly on the cast a tiny tail of white kid leather that I could manage to catch any at all. With that extraneous aid three dozen very good dace came to my net. The really big ones seemed to have vanished for now, but I proved, to my complete dissatisfaction, that a mackintosh does not make a man weatherproof. Between a short wading coat and the back of one's waders there is a small, unprotected gap; the rain finds it out immediately, and one is more miserable than if one were wet all over.

There was only one bright spot among those grey, damp hours. About six in the evening a March brown, that had been put on as tail fly for a change, rose a fish which at once leaped into the air, and unmistakably proclaimed his quality and species.

He ran out line in grand fashion, and it was some minutes before he could be coaxed down to the net – a glorious surprise: a trout of well over a pound and a half, which in shape and condition was perfection itself. His capture formed a curious conclusion to a curious experience of weather and fishing.

John Bickerdyke, *Days of My Life*, 1895

Christmas Chubbing

IT MOST certainly was not a morning for a butterfly fisherman to be out, whose idea of fishing was green trees and leaves, to be lulled into sleep by a lazy drone from a thousand insects, under a cloudless sun. I was a bit younger and more hardy on the day that I have in my mind's eye just now, and rather gloried in the beauties of a keen winter's morn, and considered a day's chubbing under the conditions of that day the very beau-ideal of a sportsman's life; for be it known to all and sundry that our leather-mouthed friend the chub is the sporting fish par excellence of a keen and frosty day, pike and grayling not excepted, by me, at any rate.

I had left the people of the house, none of them fishers, that Christmas morn so undisturbed by me they might to prepare the turkey, the plum pudding, and the various indigestible items that go to make up that time-honoured meal known as the Christmas dinner. Strict orders and sundry injunctions had been given as to the time to return, and an hour later I stood in the valley of the grand old river Trent, watching the wintry sun climbing slowly up the distant hill, and lighting up the whole landscape in a glorious halo of dancing white.

The river flowed along, curling under the roots of those old bushes, ever and anon swirling with a gurgling splash as an eddy was sucked underneath the hollow clay bank, then swirled on again until finally lost under the dark shadows of a distant bough.

It was extremely inviting, in spite of its somewhat wintry aspect. The water was just tinged with a very faint colour: a stone on the bottom could be detected about two feet down.

Chub are a fish that can be found in a suitable place during very cold and frosty weather, even when the place is not more than three or four feet deep. It is a mistake to

think that chub can only be found in very deep water during the cold weather, I have found them at all depths, when the float had to be fourteen feet away from the hook, and when it was only two feet away. This particular part of the river, under the boughs and overhanging banks, varied from two to five feet in depth, and contained some pretty fair fish, as previous visits and experiences had more than once clearly proved, and I looked forward to an enjoyable, not to say an exciting, time.

If there is one bait more than another that I swear by for the fish now under notice, when weather is cold and frosty, that bait is bullock's pith, raw, for the hook, and bullock's brains, boiled hard and finely minced, for groundbait, if that particular operation can be called groundbaiting.

It was rather a difficult job, getting that bait on Christmas Eve, but by great good luck a butcher friend obliged me with a set. The brains were well washed and cleaned, all the blood and impurities being carefully removed; they were then tied up in a square of calico and boiled for nearly an hour, until they became tough and hard. The pith itself, which I suppose I need not say is the spinal cord of the beast, was skinned, divided into short ropes as it were, and well washed and cleaned. This is all that is required; the inner fine skin is useful for holding the bait more firmly on the hook, the coarse, rough outside skin only being removed.

I have always considered that chub fishing down the streams, and under the roots and boughs in the Nottingham style, is one of the easiest and most delightful methods of angling; there is no need for all the elaborate preparation that a day among the roach, or bream, or the barbel entails. Your whole outfit, except the rod and landing handle, can be carried in a haversack slung across the shoulders. No huge bags of groundbait are necessary; no niceties of detail such as are required in some branches of bottom fishing need be troubled about, so long as your tackle is suitable and fished in a proper manner.

Besides, what can be more enjoyable than to wander along, trying this eddy or that overhanging bank, or yonder submerged bough, ever and anon with an eye to the beauties of the wintry landscape, or the wildlife of the fields, trees, and hedgerows. You can take the word of one who has been in constant contact with nature in all its varied moods and seasons, and felt better for the experience. But what is that? A huge swirl nearly in midstream, and a couple of small fish leaping right and left, tell me that something else is also on the prowl this Christmas Day. But I must leave him this time, with regrets that my tackle is not suitable for his capture. A windhover is poising himself above a thorn bush that is loaded with red berries, and I can hear the alarmed chatter of a flock of redwings, who hastily flutter away.

But I must get on, although there is much to instruct and interest one on the banks of that old river. My outfit upon this occasion was of the simplest description, although good. From that day to this I have always built my chub rods after the pattern used by a man who was the very finest exponent of this stream-fishing style that ever wandered down the Trent. I am afraid that chub rod of his made me break the tenth commandment (the one, you may recall, about coveting thy neighbour's goods) more than once.

I fancy it was the first time I saw East India cane as the principal material used in these weapons. It was in three lengths, eleven feet long, with a powerful yet light greenheart top; a balance handle, graduated winch fittings fixed eight inches from the end of the butt. I have seen beautifully finished rods, that for practical fishing were not worth carriage, the winch fittings being fixed within a couple of inches from the butt end. You must have these fittings at least seven or eight inches up the butt, or you cannot fish a stream in comfort, and it is no use trying.

This rod weighed about sixteen ounces, with plenty of backbone in it; and yet a good stiff length of East India cane has a certain give and take, that bends gamely to the most

determined pulls of a heavy chub; while the centre under the top ferrule and down to the butt has a stopping power about it that would punish the enterprising fish who wanted to get too closely acquainted with the fastnesses of his rooty fortress.

Nothing beats this cane, with two greenheart tops, mounted with fair-sized safety rings, that stand stiff and rigid from the wood, for a chub and barbel rod; and there is no necessity for it to be more than eleven feet in length, and above all, the rod must not be too slim in its lower lengths. If there is any bend about it, the top should do most of the curving; then it will hit a chub or barbel sharply and promptly, even if the float is twenty yards away when it dips. The spare top can be carried in the hollow landing handle. The two ferrules on this rod should not be less than ten-sixteenths of an inch on the butt, and five-and-a-half sixteenths on the centre joint, the top itself tapering to about one-eighth of an inch at the point. And always see that the ring at the extreme point is made of bronzed and hardened steel. I have been rather particular in describing this chub rod, as a very long experience has told me that dozens of rods are used in this fishing which are a source of annoyance rather than a pride and comfort.

The reel also in this stream fishing should be a pattern that is very free and easy running, a three-and-a-half-inch centrepin being the very thing and this reel should always be kept in good working order, the inside always cleaned and oiled, so that no check, jerk, or hindrance can be communicated to the float during its passage down the stream; for the easier the reel runs the better and cleaner can the swim be fished.

The line also can be fifty yards of white undressed plaited silk, no thicker than necessary, but still capable, when new, of standing a dead strain of six or seven pounds. If it is about the substance of stout sewing thread it will be about right, and it will be advisable before starting out to rub a bit of composite or common candle on it, some twenty yards or so; this will assist in floating the line.

These principal items, with a handy landing net, comprise the main outfit; the minor requisites, but none the less important, are a couple of pelican quill floats, six or seven inches long, thick and stumpy, capable of carrying six or seven, or even more in some swims, good large split shot. A few one-yard lengths of medium gut, sound but not too coarse and heavy, stained a sandy brown, with a dozen No. 4 or 5 Crystal or Carlisle gut hooks, a shade finer than the yard lengths, also stained brown; half a coconut shell, or a very small wooden bowl, a pair of sharp scissors, a small rough towel for wiping the hands, or drying the rod if it gets wet and the line has a tendency to stick to it, and two tins for bait; the whole packed in a roomy haversack, and the list is complete. This sort of sport is not for a seat basket; everything must be light, handy, and easily carried, as the angler is more or less on the move the whole time. My outfit on that morning was exactly as described.

I have gone rather at length into this matter of the tackle, and don't think the time has been wasted, for many of my readers are anxious to know how a fairly successful angler managed to obtain his sport.

It was a morning made for a bit of chub fishing – water in the very best condition, and a stream running that was strong enough to carry the float and tackle onward without check or hindrance. This combination of affairs suggested an enjoyable time, and something to show for it at the end.

The first place I tried was along the front of a low overhanging bank, crowned with a couple of bushes whose lowest boughs touched the water some four feet out in the stream: water about the same number of feet deep. Taking out the shell and scissors, I put a bit of the boiled brains about the size of a large walnut in the former and clipped it up as small as ever I could, then putting sufficient water in the shell to cover the brains, well stirred and mixed them together, finally throwing the contents of the shell a few yards higher up stream, so that it would reach midwater or a little

deeper by the time it got to the bushes, taking care that it sank a foot or so in front of the boughs and whirled about the stream in tiny fragments. If you are careful where you throw the clipped-up brains, and mix and stir well in a little water, they will sink attractively, exactly where you want them. My pith was in short ropes about six or eight inches long, and say half an inch thick.

Clipping a bit off about three-quarters of an inch long, I inserted the hook two or three times, until the bait was worked up the shank, and no more long ends hanging loose below the bend than could possibly be helped.

Then I stood well up above the stream, gently tossing out the tackle so that the float would travel some foot or eighteen inches in front of the boughs, with the bait about six inches above the bottom (hitting that distance nicely), taking care that the float did not travel quite so fast as it would have liked to do. This gentle holding back of the float causes the bait to travel a little in advance, and the strike, when a fish takes it, more sharp and direct.

Now this is most important in any sort of stream fishing, when the float must of necessity be a good distance below where you stand: the bait must not trail behind the float.

Steadily onward went that float, three-quarters of an inch of its red tip showing above the water, until it reached about the centre of the first bush, when it shot suddenly downwards with that sideways glide so characteristic of a chub bite when he means business. An instantaneous response from the rod point resulted in a heavy plunge and my tackle jammed as fast as a thief in a mill, which no amount of sawing this way and that could loosen. I have heard my old friend, the late Tom Sunman, say that a chub hardly ever takes bait the first time it goes past him; he simply looks out for a convenient stump or root, and next time, seizing the bait, dashes headlong round his chosen retreat. Anyhow, there it was, a bad start; the first swim down had resulted in a lost fish and a broken tackle.

Luckily the hook itself only had gone, so it was very easy to repair damages.

That swim being hopelessly disturbed for the time being, I went on to a nice little eddy that curled outside a hollow shelving bank. Repeating the operation that had led to such a disastrous result before, the net speedily had its first occupant. Ten more minutes' careful trial there failed to add a companion to its lonely condition. The three next swims and more than half an hour's work also failed to produce any results whatever, and I began to think that after all the bag would be extremely light.

A little lower downstream, at the corner of a small spinney, was a short length of old decaying timber, with one or two rather dangerous bits projecting from it out over the water. This swim was a little deeper than the usual run just there, and it looked so tempting that I determined to give it a little extra groundbait and a more extended trial, in spite of the fine skims of ice that encrusted every rotten timber and threatened to cut asunder the line if the fish bolted for that particular bit of cover. I got here the best brace of the day, both well over three pounds, and had two rather bad smashes among those villainous piles, stones, sunken timber, and old iron bolts.

About fifty yards lower downstream the bank suddenly rose to a height of nine or ten feet; a heavy flood some time or other had there swept out a little sheltered bay, into which the stream raced with considerable force, forming a beautiful umbrella-like eddy that curled and dimpled round and round, edging a mass of yeast-like foam six inches up the steep bank on the opposite corner. This swim was about three feet deep, and always worth trying. Instantly, a two-pounder rewarded my efforts.

A distant village clock, through the clear winter atmosphere, now chimed out the hour, and reminded me that our Christmas fishing trip was rapidly drawing to a close, and

that it would soon be time to pack up and away. There was just time to try the bushes where four hours earlier I had had my first mishap; so I retraced my steps, passing the succession of curling eddies, dipping boughs, old wooden planks, and rattling streams that had afforded me such delight during the short hours of that winter's day.

This time I managed, by exercising a quick and sudden pressure, to land the brother chub to the one hooked and lost in the morning. It was an absolute beauty.

A robin beckoned and dipped, as if inviting companionship, from the bush on my left; and a moorhen looked suspiciously from its point of vantage on a half-submerged bough to my right. My friend the robin came in for a few scraps of the remaining bullock's brains, and twitted his thanks in a half-starved and jerky manner.

The rooks were homing slowly overhead, a cloud of pigeons was whirling up the slope of a distant wooded hill, and a flock of green plovers were alternately showing their black and white as they turned from side to side during their flight across the meadow on the opposite bank, when I turned away for the hour's homeward march that lay between me and that Christmas dinner, for which the day and its results had given me such an appetite. I had caught six chub several well over the three-pound mark.

J. W. Martin, 'The Trent Otter',
My Fishing Days and Fishing Ways, 1906

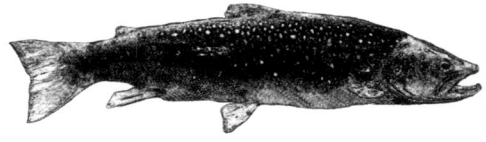

Just When all Seemed Lost

EVERY MOMENT of life, I suppose, is more or less of a turning point. Opportunities are swarming around us all the time, thicker than gnats at sundown. We walk through a cloud of chances, and if we were always conscious of them, they would worry us almost to death.

But happily, our sense of uncertainty is soothed and cushioned by habit, so that we can live comfortably with it. Only now and then, by way of special excitement, it starts up wide awake. We perceive how delicately our fortune is poised and balanced on the pivot of a single incident. We get a peep at the oscillating needle, and, because we have happened to see it tremble, we call our experience a crisis.

The meditative angler is not exempt from these sensational periods. There are times when all the uncertainty of his chosen pursuit seems to condense itself into one big chance, and stand out before him like a salmon on the top wave of a rapid. He sees that his luck hangs by a single strand, and he cannot tell whether it will hold or break. This is his thrilling moment, and he never forgets it.

Mine came to me in the autumn of 1894, on the banks of the Unpronounceable River, in the Province of Quebec. It was the last day, of the open season, and we had set our hearts on catching some good fish to take home with us. We walked up from the mouth of the river, four preposterously long and rough miles, to the famous fishing pool: 'La Place de Pêche à Bovin'.

It was a noble day for walking; the air was clear and crisp, and all the hills around us were glowing with the crimson foliage of those little bushes which God created to make burned lands look beautiful. The trail ended in a precipitous gully, down which we scrambled with high hopes, and fishing

rods unbroken, only to find that the river was in a condition which made angling absurd if not impossible.

There must have been a cloudburst among the mountains, for the water was coming down in flood. The stream was bank-full, gurgling and eddying out among the bushes, and rushing over the shoal where the fish used to lie, in a brown torrent ten feet deep. Our last day with the landlocked salmon seemed destined to be a failure, and we must wait eight months before we could have another. There were three of us in the disappointment, and we shared it according to our temperaments.

Paul virtuously resolved not to give up while there was a chance left, and wandered downstream to look for an eddy where he might pick up a small fish. Ferdinand, our guide, resigned himself without a sigh to the consolation of eating blueberries, which he always did with great cheerfulness. But I, being more cast down than either of my comrades, sought out a convenient seat among the rocks, and, adapting my anatomy as well as possible to the irregularities of nature's upholstery, pulled from my pocket *An Amateur Angler's Days in Dovedale*, and settled down to read myself into a Christian frame of mind.

Before beginning, my eyes roved sadly over the pool once more. It was a casual glance. It lasted only for an instant. But in that fortunate fragment of time I distinctly saw the broad tail of a big salmon rise and disappear in the swift water at the very head of the pool.

Immediately the whole aspect of affairs was changed. Despondency vanished, and the river glittered with the beams of rising hope.

Such is the absurd disposition of some anglers. They never see a fish without believing that they can catch him; but if they see no fish, they are inclined to think that the river is empty and the world hollow.

I said nothing to my companions. It would have been unkind to disturb them with expectations which might never be realised. My immediate duty was to get within casting distance of that salmon as soon as possible.

The way along the shore of the pool was difficult. The bank was very steep, and the rocks by the river's edge were broken and slippery. Presently I came to a sheer wall of stone, perhaps thirty feet high, rising directly from the deep water.

There was a tiny ledge or crevice running part of the way across the face of this wall, and by this four-inch path I edged along, holding my rod in one hand, and clinging affectionately with the other to such clumps of grass and little bushes as I could find. There was one small huckleberry plant to which I had a particular attachment. It was fortunately a firm little bush, and as I held fast to it, I remembered Tennyson's poem which begins, 'Flower in the crannied wall,' and reflected that if I should succeed in plucking out this flower, 'root and all,' it would probably result in an even greater increase of knowledge than the poet contemplated.

The ledge in the rock now came to an end. But below me in the pool there was a sunken reef; and on this reef a long log had caught, with one end sticking out of the water, within jumping distance. It was the only chance. To go back would have been dangerous. An angler with a large family dependent upon him for support has no right to incur unnecessary perils. Besides, the fish was waiting for me at the upper end of the pool!

So, I jumped; landed on the end of the log; felt it settle slowly down; ran along it like a small boy on a seesaw, and leaped off into shallow water just as the log rolled from the ledge and lunged out into the stream.

It went wallowing through the pool and down the rapid like a playful hippopotamus. I watched it with interest and congratulated myself that I was no longer embarked upon it. On that craft a voyage down the Unpronounceable River would have been short but far from merry. The 'all ashore' bell was not rung early enough. I just got off, with not half a second to spare.

But now all was well, for I was within reach of the fish. A little scrambling over the rocks brought me to a point where I could easily cast over him. He was lying in a swift, smooth, narrow channel between two large stones. It was a snug resting place, and no doubt he would remain there for some time. So I took out my fly book and prepared to angle for him according to the approved rules of the art.

Nothing is more foolish in sport than the habit of precipitation. And yet it is a fault to which I am singularly subject. As a boy, in Brooklyn, I never came in sight of the Capitoline Skating Pond, after a long ride in the horsecars, without breaking into a run along the boardwalk, buckling on my skates in a furious hurry, and flinging myself impetuously upon the ice, as if I feared that it would melt away before I could reach it.

Now this, I confess, is a grievous defect, which advancing years have not entirely cured; and I found it necessary to take myself firmly, as it were, by the mental coat collar, and resolve not to spoil the chance of catching the only salmon in the Unpronounceable River by undue haste in fishing for him.

I carefully tested a brand-new leader, and attached it to the line with great deliberation and the proper knot. Then I gave my whole mind to the important question of a wise selection of flies.

It is astonishing how much time and mental anxiety a man can spend on an apparently simple question like this. When you are buying flies in a shop it seems as if you never had half enough. You keep on picking out a half-dozen of each new variety as fast as the enticing salesman shows them to you. You stroll through the streets of Montreal or Quebec and drop in at every fishing-tackle dealer's to see whether you can find a few more good flies. Then, when you come to look over your collection at the critical moment on the bank of a stream, it seems as if you had ten times too many. And, spite of all, the precise fly that you need is not there.

You select a couple that you think fairly good, lay them down beside you in the grass, and go on looking through the book for something better. Failing to satisfy yourself, you turn to pick up those that you have laid out, and find that they have mysteriously vanished from the face of the earth.

Then you struggle with naughty words and relapse into a condition of mental palsy.

Precipitation is a fault. But deliberation, for a person of precipitate disposition, is a vice.

The best thing to do in such a case is to adopt some abstract theory of action without delay, and put it into practice without hesitation. Then if you fail, you can throw the responsibility on the theory.

Now, in regard to flies there are two theories. The old, conservative theory is, that on a bright day you should use a dark, dull fly, because it is less conspicuous. So I followed that theory first and put on a Great Dun and a Dark Montreal. I cast them delicately over the fish, but he would not look at them.

Then I perverted myself to the new, radical theory which says that on a bright day you must use a light, gay fly, because it is more in harmony with the sky, and therefore less noticeable. Accordingly, I put on a Professor and a Parmacheene Belle; but this combination of learning and beauty had no attraction for the salmon.

Then I fell back on a theory of my own, to the effect that the salmon have an aversion to red, and prefer yellow and brown. So, I tried various combinations of flies in which these colours predominated. Then I abandoned all theories and went straight through my fly book, trying something from every page, and winding up with that lure which the guides consider infallible – 'a Jock o' Scott that cost fifty cents at Quebec'. But it was all in vain. I was ready to despair.

At this psychological moment I heard behind me a voice of hope – the song of a grasshopper: not one of those fat-legged, green-winged imbeciles that feebly tumble in the

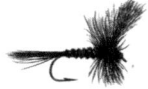

summer fields, but a game grasshopper – one of those thin-shanked, brown-winged fellows that leap like kangaroos, and fly like birds, and sing *kri-karee, karee-kri* in their flight.

It is not really a song, I know, but it sounds like one; and, if you had heard that kri-karee carolling as I chased him over the rocks, you would have been sure that he was mocking me.

I believed that he was the predestined lure for that salmon; but it was hard to persuade him to fulfil his destiny. I slapped at him with my hat, but he was not there. I grasped at him on the bushes, and brought away 'nothing but leaves'. At last he made his way to the very edge of the water and poised himself on a stone, with his legs well tucked in for a long leap and a bold flight to the other side of the river. It was my final opportunity. I made a desperate grab at it and caught the grasshopper.

My premonition proved to be correct. When that *kri-karee*, invisibly attached to my line, went floating down the stream, the salmon was surprised. It was the fourteenth of September, and he had supposed the grasshopper season was over. The unexpected temptation was too strong for him. He rose with a rush, and in an instant I was fast-fixed to the best landlocked salmon of the year.

But the situation was not without its embarrassments. My rod weighed only four and a quarter ounces; the fish weighed between six and seven pounds. The water was furious and headstrong. I had only thirty yards of line and no landing net.

'Hola, Ferdinand!' I cried. 'Apporte la nette, vite! It's a beauty, hurry up!'

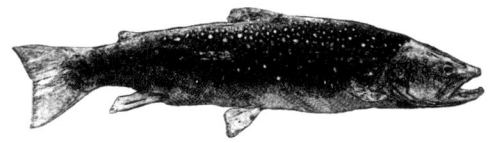

I thought it must be an hour while he was making his way over the hill, through the underbrush, around the cliff. Again and again the fish ran out my line almost to the last turn. A dozen times he leaped from the water, shaking his silvery sides. Twice he tried to cut the leader across a sunken ledge. But at last he was played out, and came in quietly towards the point of the rock. At the same moment Ferdinand appeared with the net.

Now, the use of the net is really the most difficult part of angling. And Ferdinand is the best netsman in the Lake St John country. He never makes the mistake of trying to scoop a fish in motion. He does not grope around with aimless, futile strokes as if he were feeling for something in the dark. He does not entangle the dropper fly in the net and tear the tail fly out of the fish's mouth. He does not get excited.

He quietly sinks the net in the water, and waits until he can see the fish distinctly, lying perfectly still and within reach. Then he makes a swift movement, like that of a mower swinging the scythe, takes the fish into the net head-first, and lands him without a slip.

I felt sure that Ferdinand was going to do the trick in precisely this way with my salmon-against-all-the-odds. Just at the right instant he made one quick, steady swing of the arms, and – the head of the net broke clean off the handle and went floating away with the fish in it!

All seemed to be lost. But Ferdinand was equal to the occasion. He seized a long, crooked stick that lay in a pile of driftwood on the shore, sprang into the water up to his waist, caught the net as it drifted past, and dragged it to land, with the ultimate salmon, the prize of the season, still glittering through its meshes.

This is the story of my most thrilling moment as an angler.

Henry Van Dyke, *Fisherman's Luck and Some Other Uncertain Things*, 1900

The Most Provoking Loch ...

THERE IS another loch on an extremely remote hillside, eight miles from the smallest town, in a pastoral country. There are trout enough in the loch, and of excellent size and flavour, but you scarcely ever get them. They rise freely, but they *always* rise short. It is, I think, the most provoking loch I ever fished. You raise them; they come up freely, showing broad sides of a ruddy gold, like the handsomest Test trout, but they almost invariably miss the hook. You do not land one out of twenty. The reason is, apparently, that people from the nearest town use the otter (a baited trap) in the summer evenings, when these trout rise best. In a Sutherland loch, Mr Edward Moss tells us (in *A Season in Sutherland*), that he once found an elegant otter, a well-made engine of some unscrupulous tourist, lying in the bottom of the water on a sunny day. At Loch Skene, on the top of a hill, twenty miles from any town, otters are occasionally found by the keeper or the shepherds, concealed near the shore.

The practice of ottering can give little pleasure to any but a depraved mind, and nothing educates trout so rapidly into 'rising short'; why they are not to be had when they are rising most vehemently, 'to themselves,' is another mystery. A few rises are encouraging, but when the water is all splashing with rises, as a rule the angler is only tantalised.

A windy day, a day with a large ripple, but without white waves breaking, is, as a rule, best for a loch. In some lochs the sea trout prefer such a hurricane that a boat can hardly be kept on the water. I have known a strong north wind in autumn put down the sea trout, whereas the salmon rose, with unusual eagerness, just in the shallows where the waves broke in foam on the shore.

The best day I ever had with sea trout was muggy and grey, and the fish were most eager when the water was still, except for a tremendously heavy shower of rain, 'a singing shower,' as George Chapman has it. On that day two rods caught thirty-nine sea trout, weighing forty pounds. But it is difficult to say beforehand what day will do well, except that sunshine is bad, a north wind worse, and no wind at all usually means an empty basket. Even to this rule there are exceptions, and one of these is in the case of a tarn which I shall call Little Loch Beg.

This is not the real name of the loch – quite enough people know its real name already. Nor does it seem necessary to mention the district where the loch lies hidden; suffice it to say that a land of more streams and scarcer trout you will hardly find. We had tried all the rivers and burns to no purpose, and the lochs are capricious and overfished. One loch we had not tried, Loch Beg.

You walk, or drive, a few miles from any village, then you climb a few hundred yards of hill, and from the ridge you see, on one hand a great amphitheatre of green and purple mountainsides, in the west; in the east, within a hundred yards under a slope, is Loch Beg. It is not a mile in circumference, and all but some eighty yards of shore is defended against the angler by wide beds of water lilies, with their pretty white floating lamps, or by tall sedges and reeds. Nor is the wading easy. Four steps you make with safety, at the fifth your foremost leg sinks in mud apparently bottomless. Most people fish only the eastern side, whereof a few score yards are open, with a rocky and gravelly bottom.

Now, all lochs have their humours. In some, trout like a big fly; in some, a small one, but almost all do best with rough wind or rain. I knew enough of Loch Beg to approach it at noon on a blazing day of sunshine, when the surface was like glass. It was like that when first I saw it, and a shepherd warned us that we 'would dae naething'; we did little, indeed, but I rose nearly every rising fish I cast over, losing them all, too, and in some cases being broken, as I was using very fine

gut, and the fish were heavy. Another trial seemed desirable, and the number of rising trout was most tempting.

All over it, trout were rising to the natural fly, with big circles like those you see in the Test at twilight; while in the centre, where no artificial fly can be cast for want of a boat, a big fish would throw himself out of the water in his eagerness. One such I saw which could not have weighed under three pounds, a short, thick, dark-yellow fish.

I was using a light two-handed rod, and fancied that a single Test fly on very fine tackle would be the best lure. It certainly rose the trout, if one threw into the circle they made; but they never were hooked. One fish of about a pound and a half threw himself out of the water at it, hit it, and broke the fine tackle. So I went on raising them, but never getting them. As long as the sun blazed and no breeze ruffled the water, they rose bravely, but a cloud or even a ripple seemed to send them down.

At last, I tried a big alder, and with that I actually touched a few, and even landed several on the shelving bank. Their average weight, as we proved on several occasions, was exactly three-quarters of a pound; but we never succeeded in landing any of the really big ones.

A local angler told me he had caught one of two pounds, and lost another 'like a young grilse,' after he had drawn it on to the bank. I can easily believe it, for in no loch, but one, have I ever seen so many really big and handsome fish feeding.

Loch Beg is within a mile of a larger and famous loch, but it is infinitely better, though the other looks much more favourable in all ways for sport. The only place where fishing is easy, as I have said, is a mere strip of coast under the hill, where there is some gravel, and the mouth of a very tiny feeder, usually dry. Off this place the trout rose freely, but not near so freely as in a certain corner, quite out of reach without a boat, where the leviathans lived and sported.

After the little expanse of open shore had been fished over a few times, the trout there seemed to grow more shy, and there was a certain monotony in walking this tiny quarterdeck of space. So I went round to the west side, where the water lilies are. Fish were rising about three yards beyond the weedy beds, and I foolishly thought I would try for them. Now, you cannot overestimate the difficulty of casting a fly across yards of water lilies. You catch in the weeds as you lift your line for a fresh cast, and then you have to extricate it laboriously, shortening line, and then to let it out again, and probably come to grief once more.

I saw a trout rise, with a huge sullen circle dimpling round him, cast over him, raised him, and missed him. The water was perfectly still, and the 'plop' made by these fish was very exciting and tantalising.

The next that rose took the alder, and, of course, ran right into the broad band of lilies. I tried all the dodges I could think of, and all that Mr Halford suggests. I dragged at him hard. I gave him line. I sat down and endeavoured to disengage my thoughts, but I never got a glimpse of him, and finally had to wade as far in as I dared, and save as much of the casting line as I could; it was very little.

There was one thing to be said for the trout on this side: they meant business. They did not rise shyly, like the others, but went for the fly if it came at all near them, and then, down they rushed, and bolted into the lily roots.

A new plan occurred to me. I put on about eighteen inches of the stoutest gut I had, to the end I knotted the biggest sea trout fly I possessed, and, hooking the next fish that rose, I turned my back on the loch and ran uphill with the rod. Looking back, I saw a trout well over a pound flying across the lilies; but alas! The hold was not strong enough, and he fell back. Again and again, I tried this method, invariably hooking the trout, though the heavy short casting line and the big fly fell very awkwardly in the dead stillness of the water. I had some exciting runs with them, for they came eagerly to the big fly, and did not miss it, as they had missed the Red Quill, or Whitchurch Dun, with which at first I tried to

beguile them. One beauty at last I landed against all the odds, dragging him unceremoniously across the lily pads and almost weeping with joy at my prize.

Andrew Lang, *Angling Sketches*, 1895

An Eel Takes a Trout Fly

IT IS not very often that an eel is taken with a fly, but I was once fishing with a Red Palmer, and, being tired, very carelessly laid my rod down with the fly in the water, which, of course, sank to the bottom. I strolled about, and coming back picked up the rod, and found an eel attached, which I landed.

James Tayler, *Fly Fishing*, 1888

Chapter 3

SHOW-STOPPING ... AND HEART-STOPPING

Two on at Once

TOWARDS THE end of August, 1877, I had become pretty well fagged out with office work and felt that I must have a week or two of outdoor recreation or sport of some kind, so I naturally decided upon a trout fishing expedition; and I selected, as the scene, the island of St Ignace, in Lake Superior, of which I had heard most excellent accounts in regard to fish and fishing.

This island is situated in Canadian waters, about thirty-five miles from the mouth of Nepigon River, forty-seven miles east of the famous Silver Islet and some seventy from

Thunder Bay. We made the landing on our island at about five o'clock on a beautiful evening, and, having got our whole outfit ashore, selected a charming spot in the midst of a spruce grove as a camping ground.

The next morning, I moved slowly along the coastline of our island, closely examining the bottom and the lay of the submerged rocks, as well as the trend of the contiguous land.

When an angler is in strange waters, he will find this preliminary survey to be always a paying operation. By and by I found a lovely looking ledge which extended from the shore to deep water. This reef or ledge was broad and smooth on one side, but the other dipped down sharply, and presented a rough, jagged, and cavernous face. Here, if anywhere, I judged the great fish would be sure to lurk; so I anchored within twenty feet of the precipitous edge of the reef, with water apparently about ten feet deep under the boat, but of profound depth a few yards from the ledge.

On this occasion I tried a white miller as tail fly, and a common grey hackle as dropper, and they succeeded so well that I only thereafter changed them as a matter of experiment. I never at any time during this trip used more than two flies at once, as that number gave me quite enough to do.

Well, this morning of which I am now writing, was one to make glad the heart of any angler. A southwest wind blew softly, and the sun was obscured by warm grey clouds. No fish of any decency or self-respect could help biting on such a day! I felt so sure of good luck that I put overboard a wickerwork basket, with a hole in the lid, so arranged, with a falling spring door, that fish could be put in but could not get out.

Having fixed everything to my liking, I stood up and made my first cast along the edge of the reef. No result! but I thought I saw a faint suspicion of a shadowy form or two, and a slight movement of the water just behind my flies. I have been too quick, I thought; and so tried again, letting the flies this time rest until they sank an inch or so below the surface, when I attempted to draw them slowly in. I say attempted, because they had not moved six inches when first the dropper and then the tail fly were taken in a rush, by two large trout which didn't draw towards me worth a cent, for some fifteen minutes at least. On the contrary they darted away as if the Old Hick was after them with a red-hot frying pan; pulling in unison like a pair of well-broken colts and severely trying my rather too light tackle. Any decided check was out of the question. I could only put on such pressure as the single gut leader would bear, and that was sufficient to make a half-circle of my rod. I had beautiful open water in which to play the fish, but as they rushed along and down the face of the submerged cliff, I did not know what hidden dangers might lurk in the unseen depths, nor at what moment a sharp, jagged rock might cut the line, or some profound recess furnish a retreat from whence it might be impossible to withdraw my prize.

So far however, all went well.

The fish in their fury had sought deep water and not touched rock at all. Soon the distraction of the heavy, ceaseless strain caused them to forget the glorious maxim that, 'in union is strength' and they began to pull different ways. Now I was sure of them! and very gradually and gently, inch by inch, I coaxed them away from the dangerous ground, and got them safely above the smooth bottom of the plateau on the farther side of the boat, where I could see their every motion and watch their brave struggles. A prettier sight I never witnessed than the curious way in which the movements of one fish neutralised those of the other. If one sought the bottom, his mate went for the surface; if one rushed away seawards, the other came towards the boat. They literally played each other, and I was for a while a mere spectator! After looking upon these cross-purposes for some minutes, I noticed that the fish on the tail fly became entangled with the line above his comrade on the dropper, and both then began to whirl furiously round and round after the usual manner of trout in a like predicament. When the wildest of this flurry was over,

I drew them cautiously to the boat and dipped up both at once with my landing net. An immediate application of my pocket scale proved their weight to be twenty-nine and thirty-three ounces respectively, the heaviest trout being that on the drop or upper fly. They were evidently a pair, and both were broad-shouldered, deep fish, but not very long, the largest being only sixteen and a half inches. Their backs were beautifully clouded and mottled, but the carmine spots on their sides were not quite so vivid as those of dark riverwater trout.

W. Thomson, *Fishing with the Fly*, 1883

What a Battle was This ...

WE HAD great days but what a battle was this and the angler not a man or a woman but a bird! He was operating like an aeroplane directly over our heads and about 200 feet above the lake. Slowly sailing in circles, with an occasional lazy flap of wings to maintain his altitude, and at intervals uttering his sharp, piercing, hunting cry, the osprey had a distinct advantage over us, as with his telescopic eye he could penetrate the lake to its bottom and could distinctly see everything animate and inanimate in the water within his hunting circle.

He could thus, accurately, locate his prey, while we could not see deeply into the water and were always guessing. We might make a hundred casts in as many places, where no bass had been for hours. So I reeled in my line, laid the rod down in the boat and gave my entire attention to watching the operations of the fish hawk.

For about ten minutes the aeroplane fisher continued to rotate overhead; then I observed that the circles were smaller in diameter, and were descending in corkscrew curves, until from a height of about fifty feet the body of the bird shot straight down and struck the water about twenty-five yards from our boat with the blow of a pile driver's hammer, throwing a fountain of spray high into the air. For a few seconds nothing was visible but troubled waters; then appeared flapping wings and the floundering shining body of a big fish, lashing the water into a foam, through which it was difficult to see whether bird or fish was on top. Suddenly, both disappeared under water. Bige excitedly yelled, 'He's got his hooks into a whale of a fish! He'll never let go! He'll be drowned! Gosh!' Then he rowed the boat nearer to the place of battle. A few heartbeats later, and the fight was again on the surface. Wings flapped mightily, fish wriggled and twisted and again the water was churned into foam. We now plainly saw the two pairs of ice-tongs-talons of the bird, firmly clamped on the body of the pickerel, which exceeded in length (from head to tail) about six inches, the spread of wings from tip to tip. Wings continued to pound air and water but the big fish could not be lifted above the surface. One more desperate pull on the pickerel's fin-shaped oars and the bird went under water for the third time, but with his wicked claws as firmly clamped into the quivering body as ever. Coming to the surface more quickly the next time, the osprey swung his head far back, and with his ugly hook-shaped beak struck the fish a mighty blow on the back of the head. The pickerel shivered, stiffened, and lay still.

The fight was over, but the panting hawk still hung on to his victim.

Recovering his breath in a few minutes, the bird spread his wings and with much flapping, laboriously towed the dead fish along on the water across the lake, where he dragged it up on a sand beach. Here he sat for a long time, resting. Then with his hooked beak he carved up that pickerel for his strenuously acquired meal. I have many times seen hawks catch fish, but on all other occasions they have been able to pick up the struggling fish and fly away with

it. This fellow hooked onto a fish so big he could not lift it. But there was a lesson for us human anglers there – never give up!

Henry Abbott, *Fish Stories*, 1919

Not Quite Impossible

I QUIETLY chuckled to myself when I heard our hostess whisper to her husband something to the effect that there was no fish in the house, and indeed very little for dinner, so he must take the boat and go out with his man, Malone, and get a trout or two. He said that could 'easily' be done – a fatal remark so far as he was concerned.

Being usually glad of an excuse to go fishing, I begged to join in the search after trout and Mr C lent me one of his boats.

Leaving my friend to fish round a little bay, I voyaged off with my man to the opposite point, where I had often seen large trout rising. I was most careful to expect nothing; in fact, I assured A who was rowing me, that it was a practical impossibility that we should catch anything, but we would just try.

It took us some twenty minutes to make the point, and by that time a slight favouring ripple, which might have helped us to a fish, had died away. Dark clouds were gathering and just as we reached our fishing ground, I heard distant thunder rumbling along the mountains.

Then happened one of the strangest things I have ever seen in my life as a fisherman.

A few fine spots of rain began to fall and with them came down swarms of small black flies. Hardly had these touched the water before, all around us, enormous trout began to show themselves and swim about with their back fins out of the water, literally skimming the surface of the black flies which were powdering it.

When I first saw this remarkable exhibition of monsters, I certainly thought I should quickly catch a big trout. So long as that was my state of mind not a fish would look at my flies which, it must be admitted, were a trifle large for use in calm water. But as hope departed, and I began to realise that I was doomed to failure that evening, so apparently did my chances increase.

When I had absolutely given up all hope, a fish, doubtless feeling that my despondency merited some reward, rose to one of my flies and gave me as fine a piece of sport as any I had experienced in that lake. Before he was in the landing net the extraordinary rise of large trout was over.

John Bickerdyke, Wild Sports in Ireland, 1897

A Record for the Eden

JOE TAYLOR who worked for many years as river keeper at the Low House Estate on the river Eden in Cumbria, caught many big salmon during his time. For many anglers it's the really big fish – the fish of a lifetime – that get away simply because very, very big fish are powerful and unpredictable.

To land a real monster takes skill and a great deal of luck. Joe Taylor had the skill but when the biggest fish ever caught from the Eden took his bait luck was definitely on his side.

'Yes, that big one certainly gave us a bit of sport,' he recalled. 'Mind you I knew it was something really beefy as soon as it struck. After I hooked it, I remember it went off

upstream with such unstoppable power that it took virtually all my line in spite of the fact that I was giving it as much stick as I dared – I had a powerful rod and heavy line and I'd caught many twenty-pounders in my time but this was something else.

'It headed along the river at breakneck speed boring deeply and I could do nothing – it made four or five mad rushes and I just couldn't stop it, but luckily for me it stayed mid-river and well away from the sharp rocks that would have cut the line in an instant.

'I was in the boat desperately playing that fish and at one moment I looked down and saw all my line almost gone. I determined to up anchor and follow the fish in the boat – I knew I would otherwise lose it – but then something incredible happened. and just as I was about to lift the anchor to follow the fish up the river, it turned and raced back toward me. As it passed, I could see it and I remember thinking, Christ, it's a thirty or more. It looked a yard and half long and as broad as a sow.

'Just at that moment, the very moment I saw the fish, he saw me and headed for the sea. This time I really did have to up anchor and away – not an easy matter when you think I was fishing in thirty feet of water. After that I lost contact with the fish for a while. I thought I might even have lost him, but then suddenly I was back in touch and I played him for a while in deep water before he came to the top between the boat and the bank. Being on my own, you know, he really was a fish I should have lost – he was the one who should have got away and I even felt slightly sorry for him because on any other day he'd have beaten me!

'Anyway, I was terrified he'd go back into very deep water, but as he passed the boat the next time I managed to net him – it was sheer good luck. I must admit I was very lucky because that fish wasn't really beaten at all by that stage. And I still didn't realise how big he was. Apart from anything else I'd never seen one that big before. I plunged the net in and he swam straight into it.

'By this time my wife had rowed the bailiff across to see the fish. He looked at it and said, "Hell that's more than thirty." He thought it was about thirty-eight pounds. It was dark by this time and when we'd gone back over the river to the house my wife said she'd carry the fish in, but as soon as she grabbed its tail she announced, "I can't carry that," so I knew it had to be big. It turned out it was a record for the river and it's never been beaten – forty-one pounds and fresh from the sea.'

Tom Quinn, Tales from the Water's Edge, 1991

Freaks Fresh from the Sea ...

AT TIMES when fish are running up fresh from the sea it is wonderful what freaks they are up to; throwing themselves upwards or sideways, turning somersaults, making tremendous rushes and yet not sporting a bit.

One evening on the Lochy, I was returning from the upper part of No. 6 beat to have one more cast over the Sloggan when just above the Fox Hunter's cottage the river became filled with fish in all directions. I waded in and cast over hundreds; not a fish would come at the fly, but they would, in their jumps, hit the line often enough.

After a change or two of flies I gave it up and went on my way to the Sloggan. The first cast there with the same fly I had endeavoured to entice the running fish with – and had failed so miserably – I hooked and landed a bright, beautiful, fresh-run salmon of ten pounds.

Edward Hamilton,
Recollections of Fly Fishing, 1884

Herrings Caught on the Fly

ON THE unimpeachable authority of a Dublin magistrate – Mr Porter – a fly fisher once took a large number of herrings in Dublin Bay.

There was a fish hooked at almost every cast and the fly was a black hackle or black palmer. A gentleman who writes under the name 'Storm Petrel', on the other hand, caught a very large number of herrings with a fly dressed to represent a red caterpillar, and on another with a green body, these hooking fish better than the ordinary Irish herring fly, which has white wings and a silver tinsel body. This was at Strangford Lough at the end of summer, the time was evening.

Three dozen and nine were brought into the boat, sometimes two at a time and more would have been taken had not a pollack risen to one of the flies, bolted for the weeds, after the manner of these fish, and smashed up the tackle.

John Bickerdyke, *Sea Fishing*, 1895

Thankless Task

WALKING ONE day over the horse bridge below Marsh Weir I came upon a man of the bank-angler class. He was fishing for roach and had a second rod quite fifty yards away from him, resting against the handrail of the bridge. On it was float tackle, baited with a dead minnow, and evidently intended for trout.

I ventured to ask the fisherman what would happen if a trout took the bait, and received the reply, in somewhat gruff terms, that he would have to take his chance. It strangely happened that the words were hardly out of his mouth, when the float went under, the line rushed off the reel and long before either of us could get near it, the rod was over the bridge and speeding downstream at a great rate.

Fortunately, the reel was of wood and the rod a light bamboo cane, so they floated.

I had come up the river in a Canadian canoe, and it did not take me long to get aboard and paddle after the rod, but we were quite a third of the way to Henley before I could secure it. Then came another difficulty. The fish very strongly objected to being landed, and I had no net. But the greater the difficulty the greater the enjoyment if our efforts are crowned with success; and that trout certainly did give some sport, for the tackle was very weak and the difficulty of playing the fish and managing the cockleshell of a canoe at the same time was considerable.

Against all the odds the end came at last and it was a favourable one, at least for us if not for the fish. He could fight no more and allowed me to lift him into the canoe. Then I paddled back to Marsh Weir, expecting the owner of the rod to be as pleased as I was to get the trout. But not a bit of it. Hardly had I landed before he cried out, 'That's my fish you know. My tackle caught it, you only landed it. Come, hand it over.' And before I had time to throw it back into the river and tell him to go after it, he seized the trout and had it in his rush basket.

John Bickerdyke, Days of My Life, 1895

Salmon on the Vicar's Side!

AN ELDERLY vicar was staying with friends whose house was just a few hundred yards from the mighty River Tweed. The vicar was a keen angler and every day of his two-week stay he fished for at least a few hours. On his last day he was fishing with a massive and very heavy twenty-foot greenheart rod. He hooked a very big salmon that rocketed from one end of the pool to the other before leaping into the air in a series of quite unstoppable cartwheels. The vicar held his breath and dropped the point of the rod while all this was going on. This was without question the biggest salmon he'd ever hooked and he was determined to land it. Twenty minutes into the battle the fish was cruising gently up and down near the far bank but right at the surface of the water. His great dorsal fin could easily be made out. The vicar, convinced that his fish was tiring exerted a little more pressure; the fish's head came out of the water and at that very moment, with a huge crack, the top four-foot section of the rod broke off, slid down the line and hit the fish right in the head. Despite the break in the rod the fish came into the net as meekly as a lamb, clearly stunned by the blow from the rod top.

An hour later with a twenty-pounder on the bank the vicar was back in action with his spare rod. On his third cast he hooked another good fish. He confidently expected another ferocious battle. Instead, he watched in astonishment as the fish, immediately on finding itself hooked, swam at top speed towards him and shot up the gravel bank to his feet. It was as if the salmon itself had decided it really was time to be caught!

John Rogan,
Angling Days, 1902

A Tench Caught on a Fly

HE HAD started fishing as a child. Brought up at Twickenham, then a rural backward a morning's coach ride from London, he had begun by fly fishing for dace along the shallow gravely reaches of the Thames. His father always explained to him that coarse fish like dace were really only good for practising one's casting and hooking in preparation for the only fish that really mattered – the trout. For this particular fisherman even the mighty salmon held no attractions.

'The trout is the noblest quarry,' he insisted to anyone who would listen, 'because you must fool him into thinking that your artificial fly is the real thing and when it comes to flies the trout is an authority.'

To ensure that his fly fishing was of the very best he practised his casting pretty much every day of his life. When he joined the Army and was sent to India he tried to catch the local fish on a fly – he managed several mahseer, a mighty barbel-like fish and, back in England, he even managed to catch a herring once while experimenting with saltwater fly casting.

Eventually he had probably caught more species on a fly than any man living. As well as salmon, trout, sea trout and grayling, the obvious candidates for fly fishing, he'd caught rudd, roach, perch and pike.

Then came the day when while showing his young son how to cast on a small lake in Surrey he threw out a perfect line and immediately saw a small disturbance just where the fly had landed. Thinking that nothing could possibly have taken his fly in this muddy little pond, he struck and was astonished, five minutes later, to see that he had hooked a three-pound tench. Now the tench is not predominantly a bottom feeder; he is, as far as anyone can tell, exclusively a bottom feeder. This is believed to be the only occasion ever recorded of a tench being caught on a fly.

Frasers Magazine for Town and Country, July 1852

Definitely an Undeserved Fish

NOW HERE'S a tale that few will be inclined to believe. Before I let you know what happened I must freely admit that I did not deserve to land that fish, which is why when he reached the bank, I gently unhooked him, replaced him carefully in the stream and let him go unharmed.

Why you ask would I do such a thing to a near twenty-pounder? Well, here's the reason. It was a spring day on the Northumberland Coquet, one of England's loveliest rivers. The river looked perfect, though very cold. I cast again and again retrieving the fly quickly to stimulate interest in the fish and blood circulation in myself.

I had no great hopes of a fish and had decided to give myself two hours at most before setting off for home. I was simply enjoying the feel of the rod and the line sailing out across the water. After half an hour I was casting automatically my mind very much elsewhere – a dangerous thing for any fisherman for just as you stray far away in your mind that will be the moment the fish strikes. And so it happened. I felt the line pull steadily through my fingers, lifted the rod in the most casual way and to my utter astonishment encountered immediate and profound resistance.

The fish, and by now I knew – glory of glories – that it really was a fish headed for the sea at what felt like forty miles an hour. Grimly I held on, but could do nothing to stop that first ferocious run. He was perhaps a hundred yards away before he began to slow his terrible pace. I held tight; not too much pressure to set him off again but not too little to risk the hook falling away. Stalemate. Then, before I had time to think, the fish turned and came back up the river towards me as fast as he had previously headed out to sea.

I reeled in like a demon but could barely stay in touch. Stalemate again. He sulked round and round in the deeper water in front of me but across at the other side of the river where a steep rocky cliff plunged straight into sightless black water. I began to think I might have a chance now that things had calmed a little, but he clearly read my thought for in the next instant, he rushed away down the river but this time staying close to the opposite bank. Then he did the most extraordinary thing. I saw his back and my line breaking the surface just a few feet from the opposite bank at a short stretch where a sloping grass bank interrupted the sheer rocky cliff. The fish increased speed until I thought he would drive himself on to the grassy bank but instead just as he reached the edge of the river, he leapt, consciously and deliberately, or so it seemed to me, out of the water and on to the grass bank. There he lay while I tugged at the other end of the line on the opposite bank. But I was in luck for, after a moment or two, he turned a somersault and fell back into the water. From then on he was beaten – but what a battle! He deserved his freedom so I gave it to him.

Fishing Gazette, March 1888

An Ancient Fish from the Dark

ONLY THE deepest darkest lakes in England – almost exclusively in the Lake District – still contain a few of those most mysterious ancient fish: Arctic char.

Certainly, char numbers have dwindled, but the local anglers know where they might, just occasionally, still be caught. The intelligent angler on catching one realises their rarity and returns it gently to the water in hopes

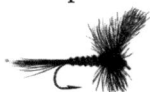

that the population may survive for a few more human generations.

A local man fishing just before the Great War caught six heavy char from a boat on this remote lake. He was astonished. To catch one or two a week was usually good going. He was so excited he decided to head for home to tell his friends how well he had done, but first he would have one last cast. His flies were attached to a heavy weight and he felt it sink far down until it touched the bottom.

Just then dark clouds appeared over the hills that ring the lake and the wind began to buffet his small boat. It looked like a storm was coming, and storms on that lake can be dangerous when one has only a small rowing boat. He decided it was time to go. As he reeled in something snatched violently at his lures. The rod bucked and then arched violently towards the lake surface.

He had never hooked a fish that felt so strong. Each time he gained a few feet of line the fish quickly regained it and gradually as the great beast swam ever deeper he saw the line diminishing on his reel. Soon all his line would be gone and with it the fish.

Endless minutes seemed to pass and the storm grew in intensity. Still the fish refused to tire. Fearing for his safety the fisherman decided he would give no more line and besides he was only seconds away from the end of his line anyway. If his tackle broke, so be it. He lifted the rod and the line tightened until the wind sang through it. Then just when all hope was lost, the fish stopped. Now it felt like a great sullen weight moving neither away from the angler nor toward him. Soon the angler's arm ached so badly he thought he must at any minute give up. Then without warning the fish began to circle the boat, diving deep occasionally but less deep than at first; at last it broke surface. It was a massive pike, bigger than anything the angler had ever seen on this lake. But why had those deadly rows of teeth not cut through the nylon? The answer – it was hooked just at the edge of the outside of those great jaws, an eighth of an inch from those razor-sharp teeth – teeth that would under normal circumstances have ended the battle before it had even begun.

Time passed and still the angler dared not increase pressure; he waited and slowly, almost indiscernibly, but closer and closer to the boat came that giant fish until at last it rolled over showing a great white belly – a sure sign it was beaten and moments later the angler slipped the net under a pike that weighed more than twenty pounds. The fish of a lifetime and caught against all the odds on the flimsiest nylon and an artificial fly.

Cumberland and Westmorland Gazette, June 1883

A Giant Pike Lost ... and Then Landed

DEAR J, – I've got a day on Lord Thompson's water for self and friend. I mean to go the first open day in February, so rig out some big baits and watch the weather. I'll take the lunch, and I will leave the drinks and baits to you.

Thine piscatorially ...

Thus I wrote, some years ago, to my friend J, a slayer of mighty pike, indeed, his friends call him Jack-the-Giant killer. Now, I am not going to tell you where Lord Thompson's water is – old pike fishers keep these things to themselves; and you need not look for Lord Thompson's name in the peerage, and so on to his country seat, because it isn't in it, and I shan't give what old Nicholas used to call my sportive readers a chance to mob Lord T with letters for asking permission.

The cheek and perseverance of the London pike fisher in pursuit of permissions for his recreation is unbounded;

and the ingenious multiplicity of pleas which he will put in to a perfect stranger, of whom he knows nothing save that he has some pike fishing, is wonderful. Old D, the well-known cricketer, was a desperate hand at ferreting out permissions; but he got a rebuff once, which made him look all-round the compass, and wonder whether he was D or someone else who had been stumped for a duck's egg.

There was a grand match on at Lord's, and old Squire L of L always attended all the matches at Lord's. D happened to hear that he had about the best pike fishing in the kingdom, but was rather sticky in giving orders; but thinking that when he got him well on in a chat over his favourite pastime he might slip in a request for a day, he laid his plans accordingly.

The stumps were set; the match about to begin; old D on the lookout. When he saw the squire drive up four-in-hand and enter the ground, D carefully meandered round till he came upon him.

'Ah, D! What sort of a match shall we have today?' and the conversation began; and D, who as a rule was a most disputatious cantankerous man, was highly deferential. The squire was jolly chatty, and D saw that day's fishing coming nearer and nearer. At length he made a dash for it.

'I hear, Squire, that you have some good pike fishing at L. I should like to try my luck there very much if you would allow me.'

I have said the squire was 'sticky' in giving permission, but 'sticky' is not the word. He never gave permission at all save under very unusual circumstances.

He hated to give leave; he didn't fish himself, but he couldn't abide to see anyone else fishing. His countenance changed.

'I keep my fishing for my friends, Mr D,' said the squire, frigidly, and with emphasis on the 'friends' and the 'mister' – 'and you're not one of them – good morning,' and off went the squire to back old D's tip, while D said something naughty under his breath, and wished he had the squire before the wicket and without pads on.

Time went over; February set in mild but not too warm and sunny. The day was fixed; the morning came. An early repast of sausages, ham, toast, coffee, eggs, and marmalade, put me in fettle; a large luncheon basket, duly stuffed with varieties, another basket with sundries, a large double hand rush basket and a pair of rods made my outfit when I met J at the Knock-me-down station on the Pick-me-up-in-pieces line.

J was tremendously picturesque, and what with kettles, etcetera and etcetera, we looked like Robinson Crusoe and his man Friday in pursuit of the lord knows what. J was a prodigious smoker, and he had a bowsprit in the shape of a Regalia Elephanta about a foot or so long.

'*Standard! Telegraph!*'

'Here, boy, give us both,' I said, and in five minutes J was deep in the markets, and I was in the telegrams, as we sped on to our destination.

At Bunk-em-out junction we found a trap waiting. A drive of three miles brought us to the keeper's cottage, a paradise of woodbine, china roses, etc, in the summer, and pretty enough even now. Alfred was waiting for us, and getting the cans and baskets led the way down through a sunken lane with high sandy banks, across a field to a line of pollards, and there we were.

It was a lovely backwater with a stage of bucks in the middle of it, and looked, as J said, 'doosedly' like pike. There were holes and long eddies and shallows, with rushes and reeds here and there, and a proper complement of stubs and piles, of course put there on purpose to lose fish.

'Well, Alfred, got any fish for us today?'

'There be plenty there if you can catch 'em, sir. There's one as I do wish you may; he's the biggest I've sin here this many a day; he've yeat a hull brood o' ducks wi' the down for stuffin', drat 'im?'

'What'll he weigh, Alfred?'

'He'll goo ower thirty pound, sir. He mostly lies in that long deep eddy by the pollards, just above the bucks, which is the wust thing in the way as can be; but there's plenty good ones aside he; we allus has 'em here when there's a flood, and the big flood last month have stocked us finely. I think we'll put all the things we don't want to use under the wall by the bucks yanner.' And he did so.

I said: 'I shall spin this lower reach below the bucks down, I think, J, unless you prefer to?'

'No, I'll put on a bait,' came the reply, 'and try the pool above the bucks;' and the rods being soon together, the tackle fixed, and the baits on, I turned downstream and began. It was rather more streamy below the bucks, and that was why I chose spinning. I had, too, a recollection of a good fish I had lost formerly near a willow stump halfway down, and good fish have a knack of always occupying a good lair. I had a Chapman spinner – one of Woods' pattern. It saves a lot of trouble and as it's treble hook flies loose, it does not miss many fish. I now generally carry three or four of different sizes and in five minutes thirty yards of line were flying across the water.

I don't mean to brag, but I learnt off the best master on the Thames, have practised a great deal, and think I do it pretty well. Across the stream with a slight splash, just to attract the fish's notice, and the bait comes spinning and whirling round in a seductive curve, as if it were going round a ballroom in the 'Walpurgis Waltz'. Once more the line is gathered in; a slight heave and a swing, and away flies the bait again, and along it comes like a streak of silver.

The third time, as I was watching it, I saw a slight ridge in the water, and the bait seemed to disappear. There was a check, followed by 'shuck' from me, and I let him have it smartly. 'Whizz' and out went a dozen yards of line. One doesn't part with much, as a rule, to a pike; but this fellow, being in a stream, was a lively chap, and made a strong fight of it before I could get him near Alfred's landing net; but at length he got near enough, the net slipped under him, and out he came, a handsome six-pound fish, like a green tiger, and kicking like old Joe.

'Hi, hi, hi!' from J broke in here.

'Run to Mr J with the net; he's in a tidy fish by the bend of his rod,' I said to Alfred who then sped away, while I straightened the spinner, it being a little dented.

There seemed to be a little more difficulty with J's fish than mine, which was accounted for when Alfred came back with the intelligence that J had broken his ice with a good ten-pounder.

Away flew my bait again clean across the water, dropping with a slight splash just clear of the opposite bushes. Half a dozen casts, and I saw a bulge in the water of a good fish following, but he shied off and didn't take. Another cast, but he didn't take, so I left him.

'That's a tidy fish there, sir. I see him t'other day just under that bush. He'll go a dozen pounds when you get him out.'

But as he didn't take, I marked him down and went on a few yards lower down, where I turned over a fair fish, but he was away directly. I cast again instantly to the spot without a second's delay, and he came like a lion at it, and I had him, but only for a moment or two, for once more he got off, and this time he had had enough of me.

I waited a while and while I was doing so, 'Hi, hi, hi!' came down the bank, and away went Alfred to assist J in landing a five-pounder, while I spun on for twenty or thirty yards without a touch.

Alfred had returned, and was relating to me the incidents of the last course, when in midstream I got a heavy pull, and, giving the fish a severe tug I was soon at the old game again.

Upstream he went, and then up again, and then, like a salmon, he made two leaps into the air, falling back with a bang,

and showing inches which seemed about the counterpart of the last fish, and brought my heart into my mouth. Fortunately, the hooks held, although he rather alarmed me into the prevalent notion that he was lightly hooked in consequence of his jumping; but it was not so, he was well hooked, only the flying tail hooks had caught him.

After ten or twelve minutes, I repeat, Alfred managed to spoon him out, and having earned it, I lighted a weed, and thought the day was hopeful. After this I got a nice little fish of four pounds, which was the lowest size allowed, but, resolved to do the liberal thing, I turned him in again, as I did a three-pounder just after. Then there was another 'Hi, hi, hi!' from J, and once more Alfred made tracks, and assisted in the landing of an eight-pounder.

I still worked on down towards the willow tree I mentioned. The stump projected out over the water, and there was a deep hole under it, any fisherman would spot it for a good fish; halfway across the stream the hole shallowed up to about three or four feet deep.

Now, carefully, carefully, and seeing that my bait spun well, and that all was clear, I sent it careering across the shallow and brought it whistling round the hole, heave and pull, heave and pull. It works into a straight line just below the stump, and comes darting past the stump.

'Now or never.'

'Confound the fish, he's either not at home or not hungry.'

'I see him feeding on the shaller and makin' the baits fly, rarely,' said Alfred, 'and judge he's a seventeen- or eighteen-pound fish. I've see him many times.'

Round came the bait again, but no result followed.

'Not today, Alfred,' I said, as I turned round to get below the tree.

At that moment there was a loud splash – a deuce of a tug at my rod point, and as the rod was firmly over my shoulder, he got it pretty hot; nevertheless, to make sure I gave him another tug. The spinner was just hanging on the water, turning lazily round on the surface, as the stream caught the fins, and the temptation was too much for him, so he rose like a salmon at a fly, and took it, and I held him. Down he dashed to the very end of the hole, then out of it, on to the shallow, where he made fine play among the small fry, then back and into the hole again.

'He'll be making for his holt presently, sir,' said Alfred.

'Can't you lean down and pass the rod under the tree to me, so as to get below it, and keep him away? If he works up and bolts in under your feet you can't help it; and what old roots and snags there is there, Lord only knows.'

At the risk of a ducking, and hanging on to the tree by one arm and my eyelids, I passed the rod under, so that Alfred got hold of it by the middle joint. The reel went two feet underwater when I let go; but Alfred soon got a tight line on the fish again, which was grubbing along under the bank, and having recovered the rod I hurried down below, and putting a good strain on, brought him away from danger downstream again; and after a little more than a quarter of an hour's tussle, I worked him in on the shallow below where Alfred stood knee deep with the net, and in another minute we had him out, a fine male fish of sixteen pounds. We regarded him with satisfaction, and drank his health, and so forth.

While we had been busy with him, sundry 'Hi, hi, his!' came down the bank, but, as they could not be attended to, J was left to his own devices, as he had another net. Alfred now went to him. He had hooked a good fish of a dozen pounds or so, played him home, and almost netted him, so the fish got off. Just as Alfred came up, he hooked and landed a five-pounder, which he returned, and then another, which was equally lucky.

I went on, and spun the rest of the water down to the bottom for a good hundred yards, but only got hold of one or two small fish. I then went up and tried the fish I had marked down. He came and pulled at me, but very

cautiously, so I missed him. As we had breakfasted early, it was pretty well luncheon time, so I shouldered my rod and walked up the bucks, where Alfred was engaged in lighting a fire. My sundry basket produced a fire pot, kettle, saucepan, etcetera. The luncheon basket turned out a big basin full of jelly, which being turned into the saucepan soon resolved itself into about three pints of fine mock-turtle soup. A shout brought J upon the scene, who favoured the soup with a bottle of old East India sherry, and a bottle of very choice champagne. How we did enjoy that soup. The day was not by any means warm, and we sat in a triangle round the fire, and swallowed a couple of platefuls each. A cold duck was then reduced to bones, and then, in fear the sherry and fizz should not mix properly, I produced a bottle labelled 'cognac' and '1834', and the kettle being now in full sing, we had just one glass of steaming hot grog. 'What's that you say? It was a shame to mix it' – well, perhaps. The best brandy makes the best grog, and if any one means to deny that proposition let him just put the print of his big ugly foot on the tail of me coat.

A comforting pipe, and then we fell to it again. I won't describe the capture of each fish, but I got four more six pounds, seven pounds, ten pounds, and eleven pounds. J got two of eight pounds and nine pounds, and lost the daddy of them all, and we threw in some seven or eight small ones.

About 100 yards above the bucks the cut narrowed and grew deep – twenty yards above was an old pile or two, part of some broken down framework. J was about to pitch his bait out into the middle of this cut, which he had not yet fished, when Alfred brought him a dead Jack about ten or eleven inches long which he had just spooned out of a ditch close by.

'Put him on, sir, put him on,' said Alfred. 'If there's ever a whopper handy he's bound to fetch him.'

'But he's too large for my hooks, Alfred. What shall I do?'

'Never mind, sir. If a fish takes it give him plenty o' time and let him gorge. I'll forgive ye if ye catches a little 'un; but ye wun't.'

Thus assured, J put the fish on somehow, and, pitching it out with a tremendous splash into the very middle of the cut, waited the event. Almost immediately there was a fierce jag at the rod point.

'Something's took the bait already,' said J, quite excited, as the line began to cut the water slowly, the fish moving up towards a big bank of weeds and rushes about twenty yards above.

'That's the big 'un, for a million. I see him lay there at the tail o' them weeds once or twice last week; he must a took it as soon as ever it fell in the water.

'Give him plenty o' time, sir, plenty. Don't worry him whatever you doo's. Let 'n get the 'ooks well in. Eat my ducks will 'e, ye ould varmint? Jest you swaller that nice little great-great-grandson o' yourn, that's all'; and the fish evidently meant to, for he laid up at the tail of the weeds quietly pouching for nearly a quarter of an hour, while J stood watching, all of a twitter.

Presently the fish showed an inclination to move, and as he was coming out from his lair into the cut J let him have it. The stroke was a shrewd one, for the pike made one dart clean through the reed and rush bed, mowing them down as if with a scythe. Fortunately, J's line was stout and new, and the tackle stood it. When he came out into the stream, he made tracks rather, and took out forty or fifty yards of line at a dash; but the stream was pretty clear, the tackle sound, and the hold certain – at least, as Alfred said, 'He'll turn himself inside out afore he gets rid of them hooks.' Then he began dropping down the cut with a short dash and a heavy drag, every now and then towards the bucks, which were seventy or eighty yards below.

'Drat 'im; take care ye doesn't lev'n get near the bucks, or he'll break ye on them piles as sure as fate, for they're full o' rusty old nails.'

J did his best, and fought a good fight, but five and thirty pounds is five and thirty pounds, and you can't do as you like with it. The fish was obstinate, and meant going for the bucks; and, in spite of every dodge – in spite of dashing, splashing, stoning to frighten him up again – he merely sheered over to the other side and kept on.

J's eyes were half out of his head with indignation at the pike's base behaviour. He'd pay him; hang him!

'Yes, I'm afraid you will; and you won't get through after all. I never saw such a dour headed beast – he's as obstinate as a mule. But he's an awful big 'un,' I said, as he laid the rod well on, and actually checked the fish for a moment, till the big brute fairly lashed the water into foam as he tumbled and walloped on the surface. The next moment, however, he was away again forty miles an hour down to the bucks.

'I'll pay him. D—n his picture,' said Alfred, panting after. 'By Gad! He'll beat me after all; he's got into the stream that sets for these piles, and I can no more stop him than fly ...'

But the next minute the line grated across the outer pile. There was a plunge and a dash; the rod straightened; the line floated like a pennant in the wind; and J collapsed.

'Never mind, old man. Take a drop of '34, and never say die. You fought him splendidly, and had the water been clear you must have landed him?'

'Forty pound if he was an ounce,' said J in a hoarse whisper, as he accepted the flask. 'Getting that way, at any rate.' Still J lamented and wouldn't be comforted. If only he'd landed that fish.

'What odds will you lay, old man, you haven't landed him? You'll have that fish within a week.'

And so he had, for three days after a parcel about four or five feet long, done up in straw, reached the office directed to him, and when he opened it, it was the pike, with his own float still attached. Alfred found the float in the water near the bucks; he got hold of it, and got the fish ashore – he weighed thirty-five pounds. Our great taxidermist Cooper set him up gorgeously, and he is the pride of J's ancestral halls.

This fight about finished the day. It was then about half past four, and we didn't care to fish after. So, we collected the spoils, we rekindled the fire, and sat around it for half an hour or so and punished the champagne, till the pony and trap was due.

Francis Francis, Sporting Sketches, 1890

The Biter Bit ...

IT IS rare but not unheard of for a fisherman to hook a fish and then, while playing it, to see it swallowed by a bigger fish, usually, in freshwater fishing, a pike. The result inevitably is that the fisherman loses everything – the original fish, the pike and of course his hook.

A letter to *The Spectator* reveals a far rarer occurrence. A man fishing the lake in Battersea Park hooked a small roach. As he reeled it in, a big perch slashed at the struggling roach and found that it too had become attached to the angler's hook.

The perch almost certainly weighed well over two pounds – very big indeed for the Battersea Lake – and the fisherman was terrified he might lose it so he played it gingerly and with all the skill he could muster. But that perch was both big and very lively. It plunged repeatedly, taking line and convincing the fisherman that it would inevitably slip the hook and escape.

But no. It began to tire and a grateful fishermen thought he might at last land this remarkable specimen. The perch was perhaps fifteen feet from the net when a long

green shadow appeared as if from nowhere. Moving very quickly it seized the perch and moved like an arrow out towards the middle of the lake. The fisherman simply could not believe what had happened. But even more remarkable than hooking a roach, a perch and a pike all on the same tackle was that twenty minutes later the fisherman managed to land the pike with the remains of both the perch and the roach still in its mouth.

Hereford Times, September 1890

Chapter 4

PLEASURES OF THE FISH

Lucky Angler ... Very Unlucky Salmon

OCCASIONALLY A salmon being played by an angler will rush at the boat, leap and end up in the very place it was trying very hard to escape, but what might look like a suicide bid on the part of a fish can sometimes help it escape.

A fisherman had been playing a good salmon for more than forty minutes and he was convinced the worst was over and the fish would soon be his, so he was only slightly perturbed when he felt the line go slack and realised that the fish was making a run towards rather than away from the boat.

He reeled in frantically to try to make contact again but it was too late and before he realised what was happening the fish had leapt from the water and landed in the boat.

The result was chaos as the gillie dropped his oars to try to secure the fish while the fisherman dropped his rod to try to help. The fisherman had one end of the salmon, the gillie the other, but the boat was rocking from side to side, the two men were shouting encouragement to each other and they perhaps forgot that they were dealing with a fish that still had plenty of strength left; suddenly, with a flick of its tail the fish bounced out of their hands, hit the side of the boat and toppled into the water – the two men, almost in tears, looked at each other. Time froze and then they looked over the side of the boat to see that the fish had broken the cast but by sheer chance it had jumped straight into the landing net!

Hereford Times, 1927

Specimens in the Old Canal

THE GRAND Union Canal at Ladbroke Grove in West London runs past Kensal Green Cemetery and is often well stocked with supermarket trolleys and traffic cones. Passers-by assume that this dirty post-industrial waterway cannot possibly contain fish – but it does.

One bright sunny summer day in 1970 one angler using hemp as bait caught three two-pound roach in three consecutive casts – an astonishing achievement from a fishery overlooked by the gasworks and dirty in the extreme. For most anglers a two-pound roach is a once in a lifetime catch – to catch three in one day let alone in three consecutive casts is unheard of.

Industrial it might have been and certainly it had and still no doubt has, a smoky, gloomy glory about it – the gasworks, long abandoned, retained the old basins or docks where the barges bringing coal had once unloaded their cargoes.

Among canal enthusiasts these were golden days on a golden (if grubby!) water, but there were always complaints that the canal did not offer a greater variety of sport – old timers remembered the days when astonishingly the canal had contained large perch and pike and even a few huge carp. Where had they all gone? No one knew.

When work finally began on the old gasworks and some of the equipment was taken down and dismantled, a most extraordinary thing was discovered.

One of the water towers that was a good hundred yards from the canal and propped up twenty feet above the ground on steel legs was found to contain numerous giant perch. How on earth had these specimen fish got into the water towers? There were no inlet or outlet pipes to the canal so the whole thing was a mystery.

At last, a biologist came up with a plausible explanation – ducks and other birds that came to the water tower occasionally had probably carried fish eggs on their legs from other waters and the eggs had then hatched in the tower tank. But what they fed on while they grew defeated even the biologists. Flies landing on the water would hardly keep a healthy population of perhaps thirty or forty perch and allow them to grow into one- and two-pounders, but that's how many were found.

Now the old power station is long gone, and glamorous – if rather ugly – flats line the canal at Kensal Rise but the descendants of those big perch are still in the canal.

Fishing for sticklebacks one summer morning, a ten-year-old boy hooked something that was most definitely not a stickleback – the boy was a novice at fishing and refused to give an inch. His rod bucked but the boy refused to give line. By rights that should have been an end of it – the line should have been broken as the fish was clearly very large. So how did he get away with it?

No regular canal fisher would have used the thick line he was using but it saved the day when he hooked his monster. Finally in the net the perch weighed almost three pounds. A remarkable fish caught in a remarkable place by a boy who was remarkably lucky!

Angling magazine,
September 1980

Salmon Fishing – Much too Easy!

I HAD fished the lower end of No. 3 beat above the Oxendean Burn mouth without a touch all morning, and then after lunch gone up to Lower Crooky. The river was in very good order and full of fish and we were all catching a lot of salmon each day on all the beats. I began to fish with some old borrowed spinning tackle and ancient mouldy sprats, stolen from the famous 'morgue' cupboard at the hotel, at exactly two o'clock. I was into a fish at the first cast and got him out all right. Then the fun started: by five o'clock I had landed six fish and lost seven.

Thirteen fish hooked in under three hours!

My tackle became worse and worse as time went on. Sometimes the hooks would break off the old flights, sometimes I would find a treble hook straightened out completely. The rotten Golden Sprats kept constantly falling off despite much copper-wire binding. The last two salmon were caught on a bare spinner, heavily wrapped with copper wire and yellow cotton, and no bait at all.

Almost exactly at five o'clock, as if the fish were anxious that Johnston, the boatman, should not be late for his evening netting, they stopped taking. This was rather a pity, as I seemed at last to have reached some sort of stability with my tackle. I might have gone on until seven o'clock catching fish with my extraordinary wire-wrapped bait.

It was during this extremely good fortnight on the Tweed that I observed the finest example why, to my mind, spring salmon fishing on these big prolific rivers cannot be compared, as a pure sport, with really good trout fishing, or even sea trout and summer salmon fishing on smaller rivers.

During this period there was almost a full complement of really experienced, almost fanatical fishers of various ages assembled at the hotel. There was one exception, however. A certain youth had accompanied his father, himself a fisherman of some experience. This boy was at just that callow and cocksure stage of his development which can be so trying to others. In the very first hour of his arrival, which coincided with the solemn laying-out of some twenty-five salmon on the flags in the hall, he stood regarding the rows of noble fresh-run fish with a cold and unimpressed eye and was then heard to remark that salmon fishing seemed just too easy.

Now among our members who were present on that occasion were two notable brothers of a certain age, who were and, I expect, still are perhaps as good salmon fishermen as there are in the British Isles.

The catching of spring salmon amounted with them almost to a religious exercise. Their tackle was utterly perfect in every respect, as it should have been, considering, as I suspect, that all the winter months had been given up to a perfect orgy of revarnishing, rewrapping and oiling.

After the young man's opening remarks about catching salmon, a look of horrified surprise changing to disgust might have been observed on the far from pallid faces of the great twin brethren as they moved silently away towards the small sitting room which they always hired, not to sit in

but to house their magnificent tackle. Later on, at dinner, this young man, quite unaffected by the volcanic rumblings from three or four choleric members sitting at the same table, proceeded to amplify and generally produce his arguments. Looking back on that happy scene, I must confess that I do not know to this day what prevented bloodshed, or at least a fatal choking fit. His fond father, apparently quite unaffected by the atmosphere, seemed to encourage the foolhardy boy. I remember that he ended his lecture by a bald statement that, although he had never even caught a roach, he quite expected to catch as many fish as anyone else during the next week or two. He even went so far as to try to arrange a bet with one of the purple-faced and unnerved brethren that he would land more fish the next day than he would.

Somehow or other the storm clouds passed for that evening and we all adjourned to the so-called public sitting room, to dry lines and flies and generally turn the whole room into a kind of spider's web. What a memorable room that was at the Collingwood Arms! There was about it a strange indefinable smell, an unmistakable sense of something very old and perhaps dead.

It was not until some years after this date that this haunting aroma was at last finally traced to its source and eradicated. One cupboard of the usual mirror-crowned sideboard had always been known as Old C's cupboard and it was believed that Old C had the key.

At last, after this ancient member had been dead for a few years, one of the other old, but not quite so old, members determined to uncover the secrets of this cupboard. The key was not to be found or procured, of course, so with the help of a screwdriver the door was forced. As it opened those in the immediate vicinity staggered back, white in the face. An old, old smell, a smell imprisoned for years, a smell savage with age and maturity, literally sprang out at us. Half an hour later, when we returned to the room, whose windows had been thrown open by some heroic member before his flight, we found that the smell had abated somewhat and we could examine the contents of the cupboard more or less at our leisure. Dusty bottles of purple fungus that had been small fish or/and bottles of grey horror that had been minnows stood in sinister rows beside indescribable jars which contained pink and green monsters that once had been the pride and joy of all the Hardy tackle-making brothers and labelled by them 'Large Prawns'.

And in the middle of these ranks and slightly advanced, as if it was their platoon officer, stood a dreadful rust-stained and blackened tin, its lid half-raised by some awful internal convulsion. A hushed whisper went round, 'Old C's prawns in salt ...'

Nevertheless, I do not suppose any room in any fishing hotel has ever heard more good and more concentrated salmon-fishing talk than that so-called public sitting room. I only wish I could be sitting there now on those warm late May evenings after days when we had landed our twenty-five or thirty fish. The world did indeed go very well with us then.

As a tailpiece, I must record the awful sequel to the young man's remarks about salmon fishing.

The next day, he and his father were observed setting off merrily in their car for Twizell, as it was their turn on No. 5 or Pot Point beat. At six o'clock that evening I returned with, I think, three fish from No. 1 beat, to find the hall practically full of salmon and a small crowd of muttering anglers. Slightly apart from the other fish gleamed a beautiful row of eight magnificent spring salmon. They had all been caught by the terrible youth who had never even caught a roach. He had lost five more. The great twin brethren had come back with four fish only between them and rumour had it that they had lost four more ... I must confess that the truths brought out in this incident have definitely shaken me. Moreover, the 'horrible boy' averaged quite as many fish as any of us during the following next week.

George Brennand, Halcyon, 1947

Salmon Enchanted Evening

THE DOG cart was to be at the head of the dub at five, and the rumble of its wheels had been heard while we were yet about fifty yards from the landing place on the upward course, fishing deep, and letting the long line work slowly round to its farthest limit in the wake.

There were no more puns now; I freely admit that I was silent – ay, depressed. Jamie, too, was disappointed; a couple of spectators on the bank were also practising the silence of sympathy. The game was up, and nothing need be said.

Ah! what a magnificent swirl. Deep down went the fish, as up went the rod, and, backache and despondency vanishing, I held him hard. The first dash of the fish told me an unexpected and alarming bit of news. The confounded winch would not run out with the salmon, and I had to ease out line with the left hand and keep the big rod raised with the right. Luckily the winch worked after a fashion when reeled in, and if the single gut at the end of the twisted cast would hold all might be well. And behold it did hold.

The fish was heavy, as everyone saw from the first, and it behaved fairly well. One ugly rush, which was the critical point of the battle, passed without accident, and the salmon was revealed – a silvery beauty that was more than ever your heart's desire. Easy and firm was the motto now. The fish was at last safe in Jamie's net, and if it was beaten so was I, thanks to the treacherous reel. The prize was a twenty-two-pounder, as bright as a spring fish, and perfectly shaped.

William Senior, *Lines in Pleasant Places*, 1920

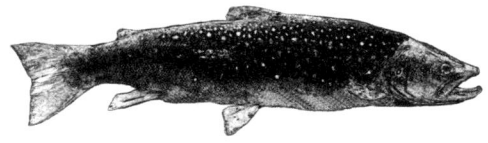

Fought by Firelight – a Fifty-Pounder from the Wye

AS REGARDS the huge fish of over fifty pounds, the first of which I have any record is the legendary monster which the Hon. Geoffrey Hill, and Christmas the keeper, played all through a summer night in the Agin Pool at the Nyth; but this fish was never even seen by the angler, and therefore cannot be included in the list of real big fish.

Nor can that other great 'fish' which a medico of Ross played all night long only to find in the morning that he had been anchored to a piece of fencing wire, the uneasy writhings of which had deceived him into believing they were the struggles of a salmon. Five fish only of over fifty pounds have been landed in the Wye on the rod, and the full list is as follows: The first of these huge salmon weighed fifty-one pounds and was caught by Mr J. Wyndham Smith in 1911. He hooked this salmon in the famous Quarry Pool at Aramstone; and on the same morning he caught another fish of forty-four pounds. Two fish weighing ninety-five pounds and this, I believe, a record for a single day's fishing in the Wye, as regards size.

In March 1920, Colonel Tilney caught the second in Higgins Wood at Whitney, which weighed fifty-two pounds, and thereby set up a record for size which lasted for three years, until on 13 March 1923, Miss Doreen Davey broke the record again in the Cowpond, with a fish of fifty-nine and a half pounds, and this record is still unbroken.

I believe this is a spring record for Great Britain. This was a magnificently proportioned salmon measuring fifty-two and a half inches in length and twenty-nine inches in girth. It looked like a massive side of bacon when lying on the slab and it gave her the fight of a lifetime before it came to the net. Here is her own most lively account of that fight:

'The Cowpond begins, I believe, near my father's fishing hut, and continues downwards for about 200 yards of deep water with a strong current through it – good fly water with a rough stony bottom – until it bends into what is known locally as the Middle Hole. The Middle Hole always holds fish, but only once in eighteen years has a salmon been taken there. It is a deep, broad, swirly place, and the fish run up from it into the Cowpond, probably to discuss the weather, take the air, and sometimes, I believe, to lure the angler!

'This one did so! I fished over him in the morning, for my father generally turns me on to the best places. The salmon was probably thinking of other things just then – perhaps of his coming honeymoon or of the vile wind which was blowing, for he would not come and join in the sport!

'I fished all day, as did my father, but nothing would respond. At about 5.30 p.m., having lost all hope, and fully expecting to have to go home and record another blank day, I was making a few casts while waiting for my father to join me, and I hooked a fish on a small minnow I had put on for a change. I adopted the usual tactics, but the fish swam about and did more or less what he liked! I believe it is even possible that he growled at me, but a cold northeast wind drowned the noise and so I did not hear it! He had several nice bits of exercise, but he never jumped or let me get a glimpse at him, and I had to do practically what he suggested, for I was unable to make any real impression on him. After about twenty minutes of this my father came along, and I called to him to take a turn. He put on as much strain as possible, and gave me the rod back again in about ten minutes, saying it was my "funeral" and so I ought to do the bulk of the work! So I went on again for about ten minutes and then we changed once more and my father did his best to make the fish really annoyed. We did not want him to go down the river any further, and he did not want to go up! We had been taken as far down as the river was safe.

'Then we found that we could annoy the salmon best by walking him up the river with very hard pulling, and then running down with him. So, we continued doing this as far as we were allowed to do it by the brute. Of course, I was constantly varying the angle of the strain, so as to throw him off his balance, but he countered this by varying his position to meet what I was doing. And so it went on, and it grew darker as the twilight faded. I had to fight the daylight as well as the fish! Luckily the fish and the river were west of us and so we could see the line for quite a long time in the twilight.

'Then at last, about seven o'clock, he got quite cross, running down and across the river, wallowing along the surface so that we could see him for the first time. Up to now we had only been guessing, but in the fading twilight we could see that it was really a monster reflected on the surface of the water.

'After this it soon got quite dark, and Jellis, father's chauffeur, had a brainwave! He has been with us for about twenty years, we called him John, and he has landed lots of salmon. He started a large fire on the riverbank, and got some paraffin and paper from the hut ready for the crucial moment when the net should be required.

'It was a desperate fine battle, but the fish now had to do what we wanted him to do more often than when the fight started. We knew that if the hold was good and the tackle did not give out from the long-continued strain, beauty would defeat the beast! An onlooker, who had never seen a fish caught before, gave us quite an amusing turn. He thought it was about time to pour some of our precious paraffin on the fire, thinking we wanted more light. There was no one to stop him, and he did it. I can smell that funny odour of singed cloth even now!

'Then my father swore! He was taking a spell at the rod, and I went to feed the fire. The tin of paraffin had been left nearby with the cork out, and I accidentally kicked it over!

I saved enough for the final effort, however, and father quietened down! We were joined by a fishing neighbour, Mr Barret, and Mr Merton's gillie, Charlie Donald, who had come to see what the trouble was about, having noticed the fire and the figures moving about.

'They brought about four inches of candle with them – bless 'em!'

'The fish, by now, was making shorter journeys, and was jagging badly – a most disquieting action to the angler, for it feels as though every jag must break something! The only safe thing to do, I think, is to keep the top of one's rod well up, and rather easy, allowing the top joint to do what it was intended to do.

'The end came with almost dramatic suddenness. The fish took a few long lunges, rolled a bit, ran, and was pulled to the right towards the bank. Jellis crept quickly to the right, but the fish saw him cross the firelight for he jinked, ran back and round to my left. He was steered in, and in a mix-up of splash and spray the faithful John Jellis with the net and Charley Donald with his hands as much round the tail of the fish as he could get them, managed to haul him out of the water. The fish was landed at seven thirty-five and was hooked at five forty! One hour and fifty-five minutes of concentrated excitement and real hard work! We played him hard the whole time with the sort of strain that will finish a twenty-pound fish in seven or eight minutes.

'Luckily for us Mr Powell, of Winforton, who kindly allows us to leave the car with him, formed himself into a search party and came to look for our corpses with a hurricane lamp, a thing anyone in our family is warned not to bother about under three days! However, we were very glad to see him and his lamp, for we were able to find our way back to the car.

'The fish was taken to the office of the Wye Board of Conservators the next day and was weighed and measured – weight fifty-nine and a half pounds, length fifty-two and a half inches, girth twenty-nine inches. The fish was then displayed in Hereford, an outline for a carving made, and the flesh was then sold, the proceeds to be given to the Herefordshire General Hospital.'

Miss Davey's fish, monstrous as it was, pales into insignificance beside the huge and decaying corpse of a salmon which was found in the river at Evenpitt Bridge on 26 May 1920. The previous history of this fish is very mysterious and the story has almost become a legend of the past. It is believed that this enormous salmon was hooked in Lower Pikes at Whitney by General Davidson and played for a very long time until both fish and angler were exhausted. At last the trace broke and the salmon rolled away downstream. Nothing more was heard until sometime later, when an enormous salmon was found lying dead in the river near Hereford. The finder measured the salmon and found that it was no less than fifty-nine and a half inches long and thirty-three and a quarter inches in girth. Measurements such as these would mean that the fish weighed in life about eighty pounds, but the mystery deepened further still. The finder went away, leaving the fish on the bank and meaning to return for it later. On his return the fish had disappeared. Evidently someone had thrown it into the river, and in the river it remained until it was discovered in a liquefying rotten condition miles further down. Even when in this terrible state and falling to pieces the fish measured fifty-seven inches long and twenty-six inches in girth.

H. A. Gilbert, The Tale of a Wye Fisherman, 1929

Joey the Impossible Trout, and the Importance of Half-Truths

HERE IS a true story from my log: Joey was a goodly fish of about four pounds, somewhat black, 'tis true, but age will tell. He was named after a certain angler because of a cunning look common to both. Joey lived in a rather narrow deepish stream and fed on a small gravel patch just below a willow tree spreading over the water; when he was hooked, as not uncommonly he was, for he was a bold fellow, instead of running off under the willow tree, as would be expected, he always ran down and disappeared into a bed of rushes about five yards downstream; there he either freed himself from the hook or broke the gut. He was particular about gut. Anything thicker than 3x, even when offered with every civility and with the greatest delicacy, was never accepted. Now, we all loved Joey, and he never created any bad feeling or jealousy among us because he never allowed himself to be caught.

Until the day of his capture we loved him, and then we were sorry for him and loved him the more.

He was foully caught. It had been noted several times that Joey, when hooked, always entered the reed bed by a particular gap in the reeds called Joey's Front Door. Mr X said therefore to himself, 'If I trap the front door Joey will be mine.'

So, one day, while Joey was busy sucking down black gnats, a landing net was quietly fixed across his front door, and so arranged that the bag of the net projected inwards among the reed stems, the handle of the net stuck out of the water among the reeds. Mr X then put on some 6x gut and a good black gnat; Joey paid no attention to the 6x gut and chanced the gnat, arguing, no doubt that, 'If it is gut I can easily break that thin stuff at home.' Mr X then struck the take and at the same time made a dash at the landing net. Joey, on feeling the hook, bolted for home, and entering by the front door banged into the net, thus telling Mr X that he had come in. Mr X gently raised the net out of the water, with Joey in it, and walked ashore.

Joey had not broken anything; the connecting chain was intact.

Joey, fly, 6x point, gut cast, line, rod, reel, angler; there was through and through connection, and all was therefore fair, or so at least it seemed to a brother angler who appeared on the scene at that moment.

'Bravo,' he said, 'how did you manage it on that fine gut?'

Mr X: 'I reeled in the line as fast as I could, got a pull on the fish before he turned to go to the rushes, held him outside, then pulled him downstream, and landed him twenty yards below by that willow herb.'

Bro.: 'How then, sir, do you account for all that mud by the reed bed?'

Mr X, hesitating: 'Oh, that must have been a dabchick, there was one about.'

Bro.: 'And I'm a dabchick too, I suppose,' and off he went.

Further cross-examination at the clubhouse resulted in the conviction of wilful murder of poor Joey by Mr — X; afterwards the culprit made a full confession, and was granted a reprieve.

A rather similar story is told of Z and Y. Z and Y had no fish, the day was far advanced, only a few pence were left of the ten-shilling tickets, the eve was cold and heartless. X and Y must each have a fish.

X: 'Now, there are two nice fellows up this little ditch; how are we to get them?'

Y: 'I know. You see the narrow place close to that rock? Well, go in above it and make the water muddy for about ten yards above it. Then place your landing net on the bottom

and facing upstream, and wait there while I go up and drive the beggars down.'

X: 'Look out, they're off!'

Bang, bang, right and left, plumb into the net, a quick heave, and two fine fellows are kicking on the grass.

Enter the keeper. 'Rather a fine brace you've got, sir.'

Y (hastily): 'Yes, it was a most extraordinary thing. I had them both on at once [and so he had], and when my friend very cleverly got them both into the net [so he did] we found that neither of them were on the hook [neither were they],' which proves that there is nothing more valuable than half a truth.

J. C. Mottram, Fly Fishing, 1921

Pike on Bacon

A FEW years ago, in a preserve in Lincolnshire, a large pike was seen to snap at a swallow, as it poised lightly over the water in search of flies; and a friend of ours once took seven or eight right good fish out of a pool at the tail of a lock, not far from the Earl of Winchelsea's seat in that county, with a few pieces of uncooked bacon.

He went to the spot – a well-known resort for pike in those days – unprovided with bait; and, on his arrival, owing to the extreme clearness of the water, and the coldness of the day, he was unable to procure any tiddlers to use as bait. The lock-keeper urged him to try a lump of his bacon.

In despair of getting any better bait, and unwilling to leave a favourite spot without a trial, he adopted the suggestion, and in a very short time eight very large, fighting fit pike had come to the net one after another.

It was as if he had despoiled the pool utterly of its occupants. Never again, even on more conventional pike baits, did that pool ever produce such a bag. A red-letter day indeed.

Robert Blakey, *Angling*, 1840

Slack-Line Beetling

WHEN THE angler can see the fish coming for his fly, he must be careful that this sudden realisation of a long-deferred hope does not cause his highly strung brain to send down too strong a stimulus to a trembling hand.

I vividly remember how I nearly lost Brownie in this way. He was a long-deferred hope. He lived in the roots of a little willow tree, and fed on a gravel bed above it; he was nearly always out and always very visible.

Many a fly of mine and others had he seen ... One day, after a heavy thunderstorm, I fancied my chances were rosy.

He looked like business, for he was near the surface, swaying in the current, but not rising. What fly to use?

The previous day, on a willow tree higher up and overhanging the water, I had observed many little black beetles: some of these, beaten down by rain and wind, must surely have found their way to him. With black wool and partridge feather for legs, I at once made an imitation, and, just like a beetle, it neither floated nor sank. By luck I put in a perfect cast; the fish rose, nosed my fly, followed it down, and at last took it close to me; I struck for all I was worth, and should for certain have broken the line and left the fly in the fish had there not, very fortunately, been a lot of slack line round about me, so that, in reality, I only bent up the rod

and hooked the fish. He was a lovely amber-coloured fellow, and my cup of joy was more than filled when, in his mouth I found two of the real beetles from off the willow tree.

J. C. Mottram,
Fly Fishing, 1921

Almost too Easy!

IN AUGUST 1927, I went to the Eira River in Norway – a river famous for big fish. On my first day, feeling rather tired after a long journey by boat and car, I decided not to overdo things and so took out a fourteen-foot Grant Vibration Rod instead of the heavy sixteen-foot rod which is normally used on a big river like the Eira.

My line still had a lot of grease on it as I had last used it for greased line fishing on the Dee.

I was fishing a pool about eighteen to twenty feet deep, and using a 2/0 Tilbouries Fly. Why I put this fly on I can't imagine, but it was given me by a friend who used to fish the Tilbouries beat on the Dee – hence its name. The line would not sink and in my ignorance I thought that in this deep water (clear though the water was) no fish would see the fly, so I was poking my rod tip under the water and watching the line gradually go under the surface, when a thing like a submarine appeared on the top. First a head, then a back fin, and finally a tail, and it seemed ages before everything disappeared and I raised my rod and drew the hook home.

I, of course, knew that I was into a salmon far larger than I had ever dreamed of. However, the fish was a gentleman and never sulked, but on the other hand never did anything spectacular, and I landed him in twenty-seven minutes.

I had never seen a fish approaching this size before, but began to realise the possibilities when the gillie, who could not speak English, refused to carry it the two miles home and sent his pony and trap for it later on. It turned the scales at just over fifty pounds.

I sent a letter and some scales to Mr J. A. Hutton, who reported that it was a male fish, fifty-two inches long, twenty-seven inches in girth, two years' river life and four years' feeding in the sea; had not spawned before as is usual with these big fish.

Neville Bostock,
Angling, 1931

Brook Trout in the Jungle

BUT THE brooks that run through clay and other less promising localities look more like the sluggish rivers which they ultimately join, and suggest bream and eels. Unless, therefore, a man has by some chance discovered that they may hold trout, it would not occur to him to study them with that object. They are bound to be found out and developed in time, since the demand for trout fishing in accessible places is much greater than the present supply, and the man who once tries it will probably find that the sport provided by such streamlets

has features of its own which are not to be matched in any other kind of water. The very difficulties of fishing, which are often immense because the water is nearly always much bushed in places, are an attraction. Possibly the survival of the trout at all in a brook of the kind is due to this growth on the banks. It is worth remembering that herons are rather shy of the much-bushed parts of little streams.

Herons can play great mischief with trout which have no protection. From the fishing point of view, I would always choose a brook pretty but difficult in the way of overhanging trees and bushes.

'Plenty of fish, but very hard to catch,' is, it seems to me, a very good character for a small stream to have.

The description of a day on another brook, slightly bigger than that which yielded me a minnow, a dace, and an eel, and much better furnished with trout, may be worth giving, since it illustrates some of the difficulties which attend the brook-fisher and how success may sometimes come against all the odds.

'Difficulties,' I said to myself airily, 'add to the fascination of angling. This stream was quite beyond me last time, but now I'm prepared for it and know what to expect.'

Last time had been five years before and a rod of ten feet three inches had been greatly prejudicial to success. For the brook winds along like a very sinuous serpent between lofty banks on top of which is an almost unbroken succession of trees and bushes. It presents a delightful little pool at every corner with a pretty little ripple running into every pool, but all my efforts had failed to get a trout out of it; though several had come at a Coch-y-bonddu, when I managed to get it onto the water after many struggles, but all had kicked themselves off before I had made up my mind how to get them out. I came home empty handed but with a great respect for the accomplished angler who, as I had been told, always managed to get a fish whenever he visited the place.

I had noted his traces here and there in the clearing that had been done. It was enough to make some of the pools approachable for a very clever fisherman with a very little rod, but it was of no use to a bungler with more than ten feet of split cane in his hand.

At my second visit I was more suitably armed so far as the rod went; I had a little gem of seven feet which was really the result of that earlier experience.

Though I had not had to fish such a stream since, I had determined not to be found unprepared in the event of such an opportunity coming my way.

And meanwhile, on more open though equally small waters, I had tested the tiny rod's qualities and found them most satisfactory. So, if the rod could do it, the stream was going to learn who was master.

There was about three-quarters of a mile of water at my disposal (so curly that a straight line from top to bottom would be but 600 yards or so) and I determined to get in at the bottom and fish upstream wet or dry as circumstances might suggest.

Here and there it might be too deep to wade, in which case I could clamber out and start again above.

I began 'as per programme', having solved the problem of reaching the water at the boundary by tobogganing involuntarily down the high bank and entering the stream with a splash and a severe shock to my system. While I was recovering from the resultant palpitations I was startled by the sound of some great animal rushing down upon me.

'It's the bull,' I ejaculated in horror and surprise. For I had, as I thought, located that animal two meadows away, and had very carefully left him undisturbed.

The gates were open but I had hoped he would stay where he was. So far as I knew he was staying there. As it turned out, it was not the bull, but merely the bank, which had caught the infection from my example and was tobogganing on its own account.

I then felt a nervous desire to imagine the sort of story Mr Algernon Blackwood or Mr Hope Hodgson might make out of the incident. There is a pool on a salmon river of my acquaintance which is called Sliding Braes, and it occurred to me that a peculiarly frightful ghost story might be hung onto such a name. Imagine the angler, in the gathering dusk, pursued by a steep bank! And then, in that extraordinary hush as I thought these thoughts, which I can only describe as a vortex of silence in which I was the helpless centre, I knew that something was going to happen here on my stream. Looking up from where I was, waist-deep, I saw as it were an undulation, an expanding and contracting of the solid clay that frowned down upon me. Frowned – that really is the word. It was literally a frown. If you can imagine eyebrows twenty yards long! What happened afterwards I shall never clearly remember. That portentous face seemed to grow upwards and outwards. It bulged at me as you may have seen the face of Aeolus bulging in old prints. Great swollen cheeks!

However, I am not telling the story of the Sliding Braes, if there is one, and I had better get on to what I am telling. The first pool, one of the best on the water as I had been told, was too much shaken up by the violent approach of me and the bank, so I made as if to wade through it, so that I might approach the next. But it was just too deep, and I had to clamber out again at once, no light job.

I began to realise that the atmosphere was oppressive and thundery, when I found the net clinging to a briar and the rod entangled in a low-hanging oak bough. Eventually, however, I was up and out and able to descend, a second time, above the pool. Then I began my fishing.

The manner of the fishing was this. Crouching as low as possible I got into position for the glide at the tail of a pool in which instinct assured me there would be a half-pounder waiting all ready for the Coch-y-bonddu. It might be a matter of four yards away. So far arrived I began to lengthen line for the cast. When line was about half-lengthened there was a hitch. The Coch-y-bonddu had come to rest overhead. At that moment I saw my half-pounder. He was proceeding upstream, to vanish beneath a root under the left bank. Drawing myself up to full height (as they do in the novels, but seldom, I warrant them, with such relief to the smalls of their backs) I caught hold of the line and tugged, first gently, then with more determination. I lost all. I looked out a fresh cast and a clean Coch-y-bonddu.

After these delays I came to the ripple at the head of the pool, got a fly onto it at the twelfth attempt and was rewarded by the sort of 'wink under water' that recalls the proverb *Ars longa trutta brevis*, which means, the longer you take to cover a fish the shorter he rises.

The next pool was round a corner. I prospected with one eye (no more) and had the pleasure of seeing scurrying forms. Nothing more happened there, for it was only a small pool and they scurried all over it. Above was a short stickle and then deep dark water on which I could see beautiful spreading rings often repeated. I could hear the plopping at the surface of a really noble trout. Nothing under a pound makes all that noise. But these manifestations were happening in the middle of a bush. Not only could a fly not be got into it; it even stopped the onward progress of a by now infuriated angler who had to clamber out of the ravine once more.

How often I got in and out during the next quarter-mile I do not know. It was very often. Now and then a pool was too deep to be passed, now and then it was choked with boskage, now and then a fallen tree lay all across it. One thing had become disconcertingly plain. The clever angler had done no clearing this long while. The stream had been difficult enough five years before. Now it was appalling. I shudder to think what it cost me in Coch-y-bonddus. Occasionally I got the

feeblest kind of offer from some fish whose isolated position prevented him from knowing about the panic which possessed all the others. But the sort of rise he made proved that there was suspicion in the air.

The whole business was of course aggravated by the impossibility of casting what you could call a line. The trees and bushes were so thick and mostly hung so near the water that the only method by which a fly could be got out was by 'catapulting' it. And that can only be done with quite a short line. I had one consolation such as it was. The periodical thunder showers that enlivened the earlier hours came at me viciously but quite in vain. Not theirs the power to penetrate the jungle in which I crept.

It would be about 3 p.m. that I decided that I was beaten and climbed heavily out to the upper air. I would have no more of that sub-silvestrian foolishness. I would go home and say that there was thunder in the air, on which account the fish were out of humour. As I went I would look into such pools as were approachable and see what might be seen. I approached the first and gazed boldly down into it. There was a trout immediately below me, and we were apparently looking at each other.

Sardonically I plumped the Coch-y-bonddu down onto his nose. He took it. I pulled him out of two bushes and a hole and swung him up the precipice into the meadow. He was a beauty. I was astonished.

This occurred again a little higher up, and I had a brace. Presently I had two brace! And then I sat down on a knoll overlooking a half-moon shaped pool two yards and a half wide and five or six yards long. Comfortably and leisurely I dibbled three more here. And from a pool just below it I got a beautiful pounder. I should mention that I happened to have a worm with me, and I may as well confess that there was another worm as well and that another fish fancied it. But all the others were caught on the artificial fly, if it can still be so called in spite of the manner of its presentation.

> If it had not been for teatime I am confident that I should have got the catch up to double figures. I had found myself the brook's master in spite of everything.
>
> H. T. Sheringham, *Trout Fishing Memories and Morals*, 1920

Mad, Mad Mayfly

THE RETURN of the mayfly to a certain well-known chalk stream in Yorkshire seems to be an accomplished fact, though one not altogether to the satisfaction of the members of the club that fish its waters.

This stream, known as the Driffield Beck, ranks high amongst kindred waters, the dry fly reigns supreme, the stream is as swift and even, the water as crystal clear, and the trout as fully educated as those of their brothers of the Itchen or Test.

In former times the mayfly hatched in countless numbers on this stream, and the carnival used in those days to be reserved strictly for the members of the club; but whether it were attributable to overcutting of the weeds, or to some other cause, the mayfly died away entirely from the stream, and for many a season not a fly was hatched.

We members of the club – a very old one, by the way – rather congratulated ourselves on this change, as, instead of gorged fish who would not look at a dun for weeks after the mayfly period, we were treated to an even rise at the small fly throughout all the angling months.

But two seasons before we had noticed, to our surprise, the advent once again of a few mayflies. I recollect putting one upon a hook and drifting it down cunningly over a good

two-and-a-half-pound fish that had taken up his position under a thorn bush on my side of the river, and the scared bolt he made when it got to him and he had had a good look at it was a thing to remember.

And, in fact, the few mayflies which that year floated over fish in position made them all bolt as if they had been shot. Then in the next season there was a more considerable hatching of the fly, and in one spot in particular a few fish were taken with the green drake.

The third year we arrived at the right time for the hatch, then a very local one on our stream; but in that particular part of the river there was a rise of mayfly to satisfy the most gluttonous of those who love that form of angling. But the curious thing was the way in which the fish treated the fly. Every now and again the half-pound and three-quarter-pound fish would take them boldly, and here and there a fish of that size would settle down to a regular feed, taking all within reach; but the heavier fish seemed to be thoroughly disinclined to take them. The bolder young ones now and again paid the penalty of their temerity, being consigned to the basket if fully eleven inches in length, or returned to the water if, as was too frequently the case, they were not sizeable.

I do not pretend to any great experience of mayfly fishing, though I have been a devoted dry-fly angler for many years; but I do not remember to have seen fish act so capriciously in my previous experiences. The birds, however – the warblers, chaffinches, &c. – were quite equal to the occasion, and took heavy toll of the hatch of these big unmistakable flies. I particularly noticed what I never remember to have seen before – a cock blackbird darting out of the bushes at intervals to secure a fluttering mayfly, and returning to his shelter to pick the luscious morsel to pieces at his leisure.

My luck was not considerable; the rise of dun was insignificant, the wind was simply abhorrent, and my baskets, naturally, were not as heavy as I could have wished. The water was in perfect order, the fish abundant, but sport indifferent.

One day I went up one of the upper feeding streams, where I had often, poor performer though I may be, secured a really good basket of good fish. After rising and pricking more than a dozen fish, all of which rose short, and turning over and getting a short run out of a three-pounder which had permanently taken up his position above a bridge by a garden-side under some sedges in a difficult position – rendered more difficult by the violence of the wind – I had to content myself with a poor brace of one-and-a-quarter-pounders, going home feeling regretfully that I had done that day a good deal in the way of educating fish!

The last day of my visit (June 10) I had somewhat of a more interesting experience. The wind was still high, though warmer, and, though no rain fell, there was a feeling that rain was not far off. The report that the mayfly was up and in quantity had brought out a number of anglers, and when I got to the waterside, armed with a box of mayflies given me by a prince among anglers, I found all the vantage spots (in the small extent of the water where the fly hatched in any quantity) duly occupied by an ardent angler ready for the fray. So I quietly gave that game up and retired to a small island between two branches of the river near the keeper's cottage. I had but a couple of hundred yards to fish, while the ground where I was standing was sedge covered elbow-high with charmingly and conveniently placed bushes here and there behind me, ready to hitch up any fly that, in the backward cast, should be driven by the wind into their embrace. The only chance was to keep up a kind of steeple cast, as the stream was a fair width across. The charm of the position, however, was that on the other side was a high bank with a plantation on it, which shed a welcome shade over the bank fish on that side.

It was very difficult to locate a rise, but the stream was even and there was no drag. Nor was it an easy matter to land a fish, as the fringe of sedges was wide and thick, and the water deep; my landing net was also over-short – a bad fault – and caused me to lose three good fish, one well over two pounds.

I spent nearly all the day on this place, and managed to hook every fish I saw rise, and that was not a great number, the rise of dun flies being so small and the wind blowing them off the river almost as soon as they started on their swim downstream.

However, despite all these difficulties and disasters I managed to land five fish, all on a small gold-ribbed hare's ear, the best one over one and a half pounds and the smallest a little over a pound; but as they were all in the pink of condition, and each fish was a problem to get, I enjoyed the day far more than a more prolific one, when the duns might be sailing steadily, the fish all in position, and where catching them would be far more of a certainty, and where even a duffer could not have failed to score.

H. V. Hart-Davis, *Chats on Angling*, 1906

A Carp Takes to the Air

IT WAS a hidden forgotten pond at the end of a track on the Isle of Wight. Not a place famous for its carp fishing but this pond had been untouched since probably before the war. I cycled over, leaned my rusty old bike against a tree and knocked on the cottage door.

'Would it be all right if I came along and fished the pond?' I asked the woman who opened the door.

She looked me up and down quite literally and paused. I was so nervous I nearly upped and ran. Then she smiled and said, 'Cors yer can. Help yerself. There's some bigguns in here that's for sure.' And with that she stepped back into her house and slammed the door.

The pond must have covered two or three acres so was really much more of a lake than a pond. But locally it was known as the pond and that was good enough for me.

Far off to one side through impenetrable beds of six-foot-high rushes a disused rusty railway bridge crossed the pond. Closer to hand the pond seemed a mass of narrow and not so narrow inlets and bays between thick beds of rushes. The water seemed shallow and very clear.

'This is going to be difficult,' I thought. 'They'll see me before I even put my rod up.' I sat on my old canvas box staring across perhaps eighty feet of water. On my left a dense bed of reeds stretched out for thirty feet. On my right the water was more open for perhaps 200 feet and then more impenetrable beds of rushes and reeds. I had no idea what to do and thought, 'I have no chance at all here, but it's quiet I have the water to myself and if nothing happens, never mind.'

I had no idea what bait to use so I stuck a big piece of breadcrust on my hook, dipped it briefly in the water and cast out. Made heavy by the water the crust sailed out to the corner of the reed bed on my left. The wind gently blowing from the right pushed the floating crust to the edge the reed bed and there it sat for about a minute. I had seen no sign at all of any fish, no bubbles, no rises, no telltale swirl rising up from the mud.

I looked again at my crust and something very odd was happening. It seemed as if it was being pushed up out of the water. Then a giant pair of lips appeared for an instant, a swirl and the bread vanished. I was so astonished it took me a second or two to react. I lifted the rod and there was an almighty thrashing boil where the crust had once been. The water positively churned! Next, the rod was almost torn from my hands as the fish took off at what seemed the speed of light for the most distant reed bed.

By now I was almost in control of myself and I held steadily, releasing line against the rushing strain. I'd hooked

salmon that had not run so hard as this nor more powerfully. Far away by the distant reed bed the fish began to slow and then something happened I had never seen before with a carp – for carp is what this most certainly was. As it approached the reed bed, it leapt from the water like a breaching, somersaulting whale before crashing back with an almighty splash and boring deep and hard once again but this time along the edge of that perilous reed bank rather than towards it.

Just as I'd got used to the moment of calm at the end of his first mad rush and that spectacular jump, he tried a different tactic – having moved steadily to the left, he shot to the right yet still close to that perilous reed bed. The reeds shook menacingly as he battered along them and then disaster – I saw his great tail rise out of the water and he began to bore deep into the roots and lower stems of that impenetrable forest of reeds. I cursed and swore and nearly cried but there was nothing I could do. Pulling hard simply made the reeds above my fish sway and judder. The tail stayed above water and the fish did not budge an inch.

I kept up a light pressure on that fish for perhaps two or three minutes while I gradually reconciled myself to his loss. He was undoubtedly the best carp I had ever hooked and it broke my heart to realise I would never land him. Time passed. No movement. I put the rod down and my line fell slack across the water. I gave up, took my hat off to that great fish and accepted that he had won. I sat on for long disconsolate minutes staring out hopelessly across the water, but then something quite extraordinary happened.

I looked back at where my fish's tail once waved up out of the water and it had gone. He must have bored so far into the reeds that even his tail was now out of sight. But when I picked up the rod and tried to make contact once again, I discovered that I had to reel in a quantity of line before I felt anything. More line came back on to the reel and then suddenly I felt the wonderfully tugging lunge of my fish. He had left the reed bed and swum directly towards me while the line was slack. It took just a few moments of careful playing before a golden bronze, dazzlingly beautiful twelve-pound wild carp lay in my net.

To say this was a red-letter day for me is the understatement to end all understatements. It was and remains the greatest day of my four decades of fishing and is a reminder of the truth of the old cliché: never give up.

M. S. Power, *Angling*, 1960

Chapter 5

GLORY DAYS

Floods and Storm – and a Fine Fish

THERE WAS one very queer season on the Kennet below Newbury, which started with a deluge, continued with a flood, and wound up with a spell of winter.

I got to the river on a Saturday morning to find things not wholly inauspicious. Albeit in a close and thundery air the morning hatch of fly was satisfactory, and for about half an hour it seemed as though the fish were about to feed in earnest.

Two admirable trout, indeed, turned themselves miraculously into chub in the brief space that ensued between hooking and landing, while several plump dace made a mess of several dainty flies which had been dressed for their betters. Then in the distance arose a dark mysterious cloud, which muttered ominously as it approached.

Having been caught in that way before, and having recently read warnings as to the 'conducting' properties of fly rods, I retreated without loss of time, and presently, safe undercover, was watching a storm of malevolent vehemence, which threatened to stop mayfly fishing for the day. It not only threatened, but performed, and by 6 p.m. the river was running pea soup in appalling quantities.

On Sunday it continued thick, only beginning to fine down towards evening; and on Monday, though the river was fairly clear, the wind arose in its might to rob angling of any small chance it might have had. Some small hatch of fly about 2 p.m. there undoubtedly was, but the wind and cold prevented any rise from anything that looked even remotely like a trout, and the fly ceased abruptly in about an hour.

Dispirited and shivering but inspired with the doggedness of ill temper, I hung about the river all the rest of the day, waiting for something to turn up. It was quite 8 p.m. before the wind dropped and disclosed a grey, cold river flowing sullenly beneath a grey, cold sky. So cheerless was the prospect that I made a movement for home and supper, when 'plop' and again 'plop' caused a hurried return to the river.

Yes, by the powers! there was a great trout feeding close under the camp-sheathing, rising with a cheerful abandon begotten of the mayfly season. What he was taking was undiscoverable; nothing was visible on the surface, and spent gnats were out of the question; all signs of mayfly had ceased hours before. Still, there he was, and he must be tried. He was in an awkward place, just in the eye of a swirling eddy, where the first fly offered was promptly drowned. It was drowned a second time, and then taken off to make room for a dry one. This swept down the run, hovered for a second at the eye, and was just about to be drowned, too, when 'plop' – the trout had it.

There followed a tearing rush straight downstream, through the deep pool, past a bush, over which the twelve-foot rod could just be lifted, and on for the swift water and the thick weeds. Here he would be a free fish to a certainty,

for there was another bush in the way over which the rod could not be lifted. Therefore, it was a case of hold tight or break.

Hold tight had it, mercifully, and he came slowly and doggedly back, fighting deep, and trying to get in to the bank. Then on a sudden he caved in, came to the top, rolled over on his side, and so into the net, as pretty a four-pounder as the eye could wish to see, a touch long perhaps for a Kennet fish, but small-headed and thick-shouldered.

H. T. Sheringham, *Trout Fishing Memories and Morals*, 1920

Battle of a Lifetime

IMMEDIATELY ABOVE our fishing was a small weir, above which lay a deep still stretch of water about 150 yards long. Herein fish after fish threw themselves out of the water in the most tantalising fashion. A venerable looking old man stood watching me, and on enquiry proved to be the owner of the field. He said I might fish in it if I cared to, but rather damped my ardour by saying there had not been a fish caught in it for thirty years, but was as pleased as I was when an eleven-pounder came along within thirty minutes.

Thus opened a friendship that has steadily ripened ever since, and thus was acquired a pool which not only suited my contemplative, make-a-friend-of-the-fish methods, but also turned out the most productive of all our mile of water.

The following morning, I went out alone, as it was raining heavily and the Colonel was subject to rheumatism. In the new pool a fish came at once, and then went even quicker, as with one fierce mahseer-like rush, he tore off some sixty yards of line, after which he settled down about ten yards above the weir and gave way to a fit of sulks, combining the reserved dignity of a Red Indian with the mystery of a submarine.

Apparently refreshed by his rest, he next showed signs of an intention to go down the river, where there was no chance of following him, as a small tree, too high to pass the rod over, effectually barred the way. At this moment I discovered a silent watcher at my elbow: dressed as a postman, he stood within a yard of me engrossed in the battle. Thinking I was into a forty-pounder at last, I handed him my watch and chain.

'What for?' he asked.

'You don't mean to say you're going to try and follow him?'

'I most assuredly am,' was my reply. 'If that fish goes down, I'm going too.'

'Hold on for three minutes for any sake,' he answered and doubled away to a cottage, whence he shortly returned breathless with a saw.

Then commenced an epic: the postman sawed like grim death: the fish fought like the devil: inch by inch he fell back to the rush of water over the weir: and I for my part held on as I never held on to a fish before. Which would give first it was impossible to say.

'He's going,' I cried at last as the salmon turned, and availing himself of the heavy current, went off as though my stout greenheart rod had been a lady's riding whip: in another second I should have followed into the water, when in the very act of doing so a crack like a pistol shot proclaimed the fall of the tree, By this time my servant had joined the glad throng, and by combining forces with the postman, pulled the tops of the trees down till they just, just, enabled me to pass the rod over.

Two stone walls and a blackthorn hedge were negotiated in a manner which would have done credit to a competitor for the Conyngham Cup, but a trip in a drain proved disastrous

to the favourite, and put me into the river up to my waist. No sooner in than out and away again as madly as before.

An elder bush had to be pulled up by the roots by my rapidly swelling cortège, and that brought us to the Rubicon, a long bridge, half a mile from where the fish had been hooked. No ordinary bridge either, but one of some dozen arches, every one of them, except the far one, with a wire stretched across it festooned with weeds, and down the far one, selected by the fish, some six feet of rushing black water.

He got within ten yards of salvation, and then something induced him to turn and have another sulk. But by now I had been with him just one hour, and by sheer force pulled him over to my side, when that noble-minded postman rushed into three feet of water, took a fleeting chance with the net, and triumphantly bore him into the field. And was he a forty-pounder? No. Was he thirty? No. Was he twenty? No: he was eighteen, but instead of being in his mouth, the hook had been in his pectoral fin all the time, which, of course, accounted for his prolonged resistance.

But in terms of battle, excitement and sheer good fortune, this was the finest bout I ever had with a salmon, and when the postman went off he altogether forgot to return me my gold watch. But it could not have been safer in the Bank of England, for that day commenced a friendship which has never known a cloud in all these years. Oh! excellent Garrett; easily could I fill a book with you and your anecdotes and sayings: your scorn for bunglers and your admiration for artists: your knowledge of the river and your love for the little red shrimps from Galway.

On one occasion he was fishing with my wife, and I came on them from behind sitting silent side by side gazing into the river.

'You're very quiet, you two,' I ventured to remark.

'We're just cogitating – like the eels in the mud,' was his astonishing reply.

Arthur Mainwaring, *Fishing and Philandering*, 1914

Betrayed by a Reel

WHATEVER YOU do, have nothing to say to multiplying reels: they are apt to betray you in the hour of trial.

My first discovery of their insufficiency for heavy fish created some embarrassment at the time. I had a pet multiplier, which ran beautifully, and which I had long used for trout fishing. As it was sufficiently large to contain a salmon line, I employed it for that purpose also, till it began to get rickety with the more heavy work.

One day, the water being fallen in, and the morning also being sunny, so as to exclude the expectation of landing a salmon, I put some trout tackle at the end of my line, which was on the said reel, and began trouting in Boleside water.

In the course of the day a cloud passed before the sun; and at the same time, as is usually the case, a slight breeze arose and ruffled the surface of the water. I hastened to change my tackle, and substituted a small salmon fly in place of the trout ones: small, because, as I have said, the water was quite fallen in.

Though many years have passed over my head since that time, I remember this fly well. His wings were of the clear brown feather from the bittern; his body of black wool, with a hackle of the same colour; and his tail of a very pronounced yellow, being made of the feather of a golden pheasant; red he was in the head, and altogether of a very commendable and alluring aspect.

The curl on the water still continuing, I whisked him off gaily. At the very second throw, the pool being somewhat dead, I saw the water heave up, advancing in a wave towards me. I waited patiently for the break, which was a slight one, but pleasant and beauteous to behold. This I knew to be the act of the *Salmo salar*; and as my line was short, I was, as

I before recommended to others, in no hurry to strike; but fix him I did in due season. He no sooner felt the hook than he began to rebel; and executed some very heavy runs, which so disconcerted the machinery of my multiplier as almost to dislocate the wheels. The line gave out with starts and hitches, so that I was obliged to assist it with my hands. To wind up it resolutely refused; so that I was compelled to gather in the line in large festoons when it was necessary to shorten it, and again to give these out as best I could when the fish made a run. Add to this embarrassment that the ground was distressing, there being alder bushes in my rear, which made it impossible for me to retreat and advance by land, by which means I could have humoured the fancies of the fish, so as to obviate in some degree the necessity of giving out and shortening the line. So I had no power whatever over the salmon, which was evidently a very large one.

In the course of an hour, I made no impression upon him at all, my whole aim being to avoid a break. I never engaged with a more subtle animal.

Sometimes he would make the tour of all the neighbouring stones, where he endeavoured, no doubt, to rub the hook out of his mouth; then he would take a long rest, as if he cared nothing about it.

From the cause I have mentioned my tackle was always in disorder, which kept me in great apprehension. Thus, the matter went on for nearly two hours more, still with a very dubious result. At length a stone being thrown in by my attendant at a spot where I could follow along the bank, he put his head down the river peremptorily, and went off like

a rocket. I ran with him down the channel, as he skimmed through the shallows and darted through the rough gorges, in evident danger, as I was, of losing him every moment. At length he fairly exhausted himself, and I was able to urge him to a sandbank, and lay him on his broadside.

The sandbank, however, had a few inches of water running over it, but not sufficient to cover the fish. My attendant, Philip Garrat, had the tact to place himself between the deep water and the fish. Then came the struggle. A Wiltshire novice, like the said Philip, could not hold a live salmon with his hands, so he tried to throw him forward on the dry channel. All this time I hallooed stoutly to him to take care of the line. My anxiety was extreme; for the fish was sometimes able to place himself in a swimming posture, and wriggle away near the deep water. In fact, had there been but one inch of water more over the sandbank, he would have had it all his own way. Philip, aware of the danger, set at him with redoubled activity, scooping and kicking his fastest and best. But the event being still doubtful, he knelt down and grappled with him; and finding him still slippery and elusive, he cast himself bodily upon him, and fixed him with his weight at once. Whatever he might have thought, he only said, looking up with a grin of delight and with a Wiltshire accent, 'I got un – be hanged if I ha'nt.'

A cold bath for a few minutes more or less is of no consequence; so I made him remain till I came up and gripped the huge salmon by the tail, and walked to dry land with him, triumphant.

I was nearly three hours in landing this fish, all owing to the derangement of a multiplying reel; but my success is a reminder that good fortune may smile on us in the end, as that splendid salmon can testify.

William Scrope, Days and Nights of Salmon Fishing in the Tweed, 1854

A Grumpy Gillie on the Dee

I WAS the guest of a boy whose father was tenant of a fine stretch of the Dee. Early in the morning we were met at the riverside by a tall and shaggy gamekeeper; taciturn, businesslike; not ill-natured to look at, but certainly not so cheerful as many a gillie is; resentful, I have no doubt, at having to attend on youngsters.

When he saw my rod, that with which I had been successful on the Eden, his frown deepened into irritated contempt. I had come to think my rod, which was of greenheart and thirteen feet long, sufficient for all occasions. If I could manage a salmon in one part of the country, what had I to fear in any other? Thus, I had proudly reasoned, if at all, in setting out for Banchory. My satisfaction, it seemed, was foolish. Not speaking a word, the gamekeeper held out a hand for the rod, and, with a wave of the other, called my snubbed consideration to the grassy bank behind him. There lay two rods, salmon rods, with huge reels, lines run through the rings, and enormous flies ready to be used. I had never before fired a salmon fly in earnest; but with that majestic Highlandman looking on, still silent, and not complimentary in spirit, this was no time to seem confused or hesitant.

Calmly, therefore, with aplomb, I stooped towards one of the rods. It was much less easy to lift than I could have supposed, but with an effort, while the gillie's back was turned towards me, soon I had it erect. Holding it against my right shoulder I stepped over the pebbles, steadily as I could to the water's edge. What was to be done next? The salmon were rising just in front of me. I saw them, I had never seen so many in one pool before, and I have never had such a spectacle since. They were not leaping. Merely they were constantly coming up, gently breaking the water with their heads, and in some cases, as they dropped, making swirls with their tails.

They were exactly like gigantic trout feeding in a well-stocked pool. There was I standing gazing at them, inactive. That, however, was not for more than a minute. I knew that the discomforting visage of the Highlandman in the rear would be upon me and that it was not a white feather I held aloft. To work, then!

Cautiously I let the long rod droop; unloosed the very large fly; with help from the torrent, let out a good many yards of line; and was prepared for action. I cast; it had been a sound intuition which made me hesitate. A salmon rod, even if it be an inheritance from times gone by, is not of insupportable weight; but if it be of the Shannon build, heavier in the middle than at the butt, it calls for a skill in balancing that is not yours by nature.

Just as I saw the fly about to fall into the thick of the fish, about twenty yards out, I felt my bodily equilibrium being not less disturbed than the mental. The great rod, with the fat knob at the end wedged against the pit of my person was a lever. Headfirst, I followed it into the river. As the pebble bank was shelving, the water into which I went was not deep. I remember wishing that it were. Death by honourable drowning would be preferable to be beholding again the countenance of that Highlandman. His shaggy cheeks would now be relaxed in sarcasm. He helped me out and that by the ignominious heels.

When I was once more upstanding, 'You should go home,' he said, not ungently; his tenderness was cutting. Home indeed! Still, I could not well begin again just there. Yearning for solitude, to be unseen, I wandered off in the direction of Balmoral, leaving my host and the Gael to make the best they could of Banchory. I did not go far. Within a quarter of a mile I came upon a temptation. A ledge of scraggy rock stretched out into the river, from the point of this natural pier, I should be able, with ease, to cast upon an attractive patch of water.

Thither I picked my way, and then let out the line. At the very first cast, delivered with desperate resolution, I found

myself in trouble, which, though less unheroic, was more serious than that from which I had just emerged. In the black water, where the fly was stemming the strong current, I saw a heaving gleam from out the depths, and instinctively raised the rod. Lo! I had hooked a salmon. At first his behaviour was sedate; he ran across towards the other bank and slowly returned to his holt. Then, after a pause as if for reflection, he began a movement straight towards me. He came as it were foot by foot, deviating neither to the right nor to the left; I reeling up in strict accordance with his leisure; deliberately he came, until he was at my very toes, in the dark depths gurgling in the lee of the perilous jetty.

There he rested; to keep in touch with him, I had to hold the rod straight up, sometime, as it moved slightly, or as I did, the taut line brushed my face. For many minutes the fish lay still, how long was this to go on? The query was not without dire suggestiveness. While the salmon sulked, I realised, I should, unless I took action, be imprisoned on the damp, cold, uncomfortable Dee. There was no one looking, I would make a bolt for freedom. The ledge of rock was so narrow and so scraggy that I had had much difficulty in walking over it when comparatively unencumbered; but it was just possible that if I ran in bold long bounds fortune would favour my footsteps. Holding the rod so that the winch would be free to act, cautiously I wheeled right about face, and made for the shore in haste. When I was halfway to safety the salmon turned tail and fled, and of course, my risky foothold failed. The fish was going downstream, and keeping well in towards our own side of the river, which, in water much deeper than myself could measure, helped me to keep afloat and gain a footing. There was now no lack of liveliness in the proceeding.

The line whizzed hither and thither through the broad flood; it was wagged in violent jerks from side to side; the salmon leapt again and again, and his splashings were heard above the breeze. Suddenly at a bend of the tree-fringed bank

I came within sight of the Highlandman and my host. In the river and not well-groomed, I alone, it would appear, was for the moment visible.

'Damnation! here he is again,' I heard the Highlandman exclaim. Instantly, however, seeing things truly, he changed his tune; 'Reel in, reel in!' he cried, 'or she'll be roond that rock and cut ye!' I saw the risk. Although manifestly affected by what had befallen, the salmon, head to the torrent, was moving steadily, sideways, towards the other bank, near which a jagged rock churned the water into foam. If he won his way beyond it on the upper side, and then dropped down, I should be undone. With all my might I checked him; rod, line, and cast stood the uncompromising strain; desisting, the salmon rolled over and over, as if in rage, lashing the water with his tail; and ere long, almost at the very spot where little more than an hour before he had landed the fisherman, the Highlandman landed the fish.

W. Earl Hodgson, *Salmon Fishing*, 1906

Fish from a Ruined Swim

ONE OF the strangest adventures I ever had when fishing was in the early morning of a glorious but hot August bank holiday. A friend named Spinks and myself had made arrangements to go to a famous spot on the middle Trent.

A night or two previously we had clipped up nearly a thousand big lobworms and scattered them down the swim, the condition of the water being favourable for worm fishing.

Everything pointed to a very successful day; the only thing was, could we get there early enough to have an

uninterrupted use of the swim? Unfortunately, I found my friend had overslept himself, and we were an hour and a half later in starting than the time arranged for. Spinks had another friend, a very small chap, who rejoiced in the name of Little Tich; he was Spinks' assistant in the ironworks.

This little man was gone on fishing, but he had no judgement worth the name. He begged so hard to be one of the party, that we had not the heart to refuse. Now as it happened the little man was early, and so he trudged along to the river. Arriving there, he waited patiently for an hour, and it being a very hot morning and he a born swimmer, he plunged in; and when we arrived on the scene, there he was splashing up and down the very swim we had baited.

The flow of language that Spinks treated his mate to was more forcible than polite; finally, he made him swim over to the other side of the river, threatening to bombard him with stones if he dared to come our side for an hour. Here was a nice 'how do you do'. We expected that swim was utterly ruined, but it turned out better than we thought; towards evening we got a wonderful bag, consisting of big roach, dace, chub, and splendid bream. But one lesson was learned: our small friend never bathed in a baited swim again.

J. W. Martin, 'The Trent Otter',
My Fishing Days and Fishing Ways, 1906

Tied and Tangled

WITHIN TEN minutes of the sluice being opened, and the old waterwheel revolving, then every trout in the place was mad on, eagerly looking out for any stray scraps swept down by the oncoming flood.

Once or twice during the season the friendly miller would drop me a note to say the sluices would be opened, and as the opportunity was too good to be wantonly lost, something very desperate had to be the matter if I failed to go.

At the particular time of which I write I found, on arriving at the scene of operations, the mill dam in front full to the brim, while the *clank, clank* of the ancient waterwheel proclaimed the fact that water was just beginning to trickle down the little stream below. Getting to work with as little delay as possible in the small pool at the foot of the wheel, with the tail end of a lobworm, I had a brace of fighting fit one-pounders safely netted inside twenty minutes. This was decidedly good business, raising hopes of a fine afternoon's sport, which the subsequent result amply justified.

After leaving the tail of the mill there was rather a long stretch of unproductive water, which never seemed to hold any fish at all. An abrupt corner, where the water ran alongside a row of brambles, probably a couple of feet deep and about the same width, next claimed attention; here three half-pounders, lusty and strong, were safely landed. A little lower down a willow projected right over the water, with its encircling arms spreading about in every direction, and here I had the first mishap of the afternoon.

Right under this willow was a likely pool, very small, it was true; it took me fully ten minutes to persuade that worm to go properly into the right place, and once there it only required about two more seconds to finish the job and hasten the catastrophe. A fine trout, on being hooked, at once sprang upwards, dropped

over the other side of a bough, hung there for a second, then gave another upward jerk, and like a shadow vanished into the pool from which he came. I had to repair damages after that, and go lower downstream in search of further adventures.

A tiny cascade over a rocky bottom, were the stream dropped a few inches over a series of small ledges, next claimed attention; this was one of the most certain places for sport and breakages in the whole length of the water.

Just here, on the opposite side, the bank rose steep and abrupt some ten or eleven feet above the waterline; this bank was a series of stone shelves or layers piled one above another with remarkable regularity. They looked as though they had been built there by human hands in the days long past, the cracks and crevices between the stones being inhabited by all sorts of spiders, tiny beetles, and other insects. While examining this living colony a kingfisher plopped out of a hole within a foot of my head with startling suddenness, and, uttering his shrill cry of alarm, flitted down the brook like a living gem. I poked the thin end of my landing handle into that hole, but could not reach the end of it; if anyone had wanted that nest it would have required a heavy charge of dynamite to have blown up the solid rocks, as my landing net went into the crevice at least two feet.

A little below one of these tiny waterfalls a big stone stuck up out of the water, forming a pool not more than eighteen inches deep and less than a yard across it. This pool gave me the best trout of the afternoon, a grand fish of nearly two pounds. Hereabouts were twenty yards of capital water, which yielded no fewer than five of my best ever fish; but the surroundings were so cramped, and the bushes so much in evidence, together with the gloom caused by some thick overhanging trees, that a considerable amount of crawling and snake-like progression had to be indulged in before I got those five fish safely landed. The afternoon was wearing on, and there were still a few good places to try; but all at once I found the water suddenly grow less and less, and finally it died away altogether, telling me that my friend the miller had exhausted his water supply, and that the game, as far as that afternoon was concerned, was up. But what a wonderful afternoon it had been.

In fishing these tiny streams I always preferred a short stumpy quill float; a friend of mine, who accompanied me once or twice to a similar brook, used to use a very small bullet and no float, but I fancied more than once that he handicapped himself sadly, as in using a small leger bullet he had to throw the bait direct to where he wanted it, and chance getting it hung up over the jungle of bushes; whereas in many cases the float could be swum and worked down an extra yard or two under the very fastnesses, where the bullet could not be pitched. Tackle should always be fine, but strong, chub gut being about right. Wasp grubs and a bunch of maggots are also good baits for this fishing, but I always fancied when the fresh water ran from the mill the tail end of a lob was decidedly the most attractive.

If the water is only an ordinary stream, not affected by the mill water, then wasp grubs and caddis baits would be better, reserving worms for a clouded water after heavy rains.

That afternoon I had landed seventeen splendid trout that together weighed more than eleven pounds – a very good result on a snag-filled overgrown stream.

In all probability some of my readers know of a similar place, where at first sight they would not dream of catching trout or anything else. I can call to mind half a dozen similar brooks. Once in particular an old friend rated me soundly when I took him to one of them for a day's sport; but he altered his tune at day's end. If by chance there is a good river in the immediate vicinity – be it trout stream, or chub, or dace, or roach, with an outlet from or inlet into it – the tiny little brook that looks so insignificant might astonish him.

On that evening, after leaving the riverbank, I went home fully satisfied with my outing – and I longed that the time would soon come round when the friendly miller would again send me his welcome note.

J. W. Martin, 'The Trent Otter',
My Fishing Days and Fishing Ways, 1906

Everything Comes to Him who Waits

THERE WAS one spot down the Lower Trent where the water was twelve feet deep, and suddenly shoaled up to seven feet, forming a sort of hollow bank or shelf right across the channel of the river. That was an easy place to get our groundbait worms in; the bulk would lodge under that old ledge. We often wondered what that old ledge was; sometimes we thought it must have been some old timber ship silted completely up.

It was a terror of a place to fish; you never knew when to catch it at a right height. If we found it right so that we could run the long-cork float right under the ledge, and it would stop there ten minutes, we were bound to get a good barbel; but more often than not it completely baffled us, so curious was the swim.

I have gone before daybreak in the morning to throw in worms for the barbel swim. I have gone at sunset and put many thousands in; have baited the runs and weir pools and streams with a bag of boiled-up greaves; have legered, long-corked, and floated with worms, caddis, greaves, and maggots; and now I say again, the game was hardly worth the candle.

But who has felt the boring tugs of one of those powerful fish, as he has fought it out to the bitter end; and when he has been landed, within ten minutes has had the same experience again with another fish: now and again, after a ten minutes' fight that will live in his memory, getting one that he is tempted to put in a glass case; or has felt the weakened tackle give way at a knot, and the fish of the day is gone — who has experienced these things and not succumbed to the charms of barbel fishing?

These experiences only come sometimes; the blanks are more numerous than the prizes. But still you keep going until another day; probably a couple of seasons later you are down the Trent, or up the Kennet, or at Old Windsor Weir, or round Penton Hook; and at night, when you look at the dozen splendid barbel that have fallen during the day to your own rod, you wonder how anybody can say fishing is an ignoble sport. That bag compensates for all, and you are ready to say the same as I say, who have had the experience, that barbel fishing, when fish are on, is a sport of the very highest class.

It was a six-pound barbel that once, a good many years ago, nearly betrayed me. My old friend Frank Sims was a believer in night fishing when water was bright and low, legering with a good lump of white greaves. We went one night to a deep hole not far from Kelham Bridge, on the Trent; I got a six-pounder that fought and splashed in the darkness like a fury. The water had hardly settled after all this commotion when we heard the tramp of the keeper along the gravel. We had no business there at night. Fortunately, we were under an overhanging bank, and the keeper had to make a detour above us. Just at that moment my big barbel gave a hoarse, sucking croak, enough to attract attention at such a short distance.

The keeper stopped, and appeared to listen for a minute, but hearing nothing further went on. It was a narrow escape. We got five barbel and a big chub that evening; the chub was the smallest, and it was an ounce or two over four pounds.

Between Carlton Mill and the osier holt, down the Lower Trent, there was one of the loveliest barbel eddies it was ever my good fortune to fish. Old Trent men will know the very spot; it was in the last meadow before you reached the osiers, and a lot of rough stones edged the river's brink just there. The depth in those days varied from six to ten feet; and a long, oily eddy curled away right under the very shadow of those old willows. A gentleman from Sheffield was down, and he particularly wanted his first essay among the barbel to be

successful; so to ensure that end sent me down a couple of thousand lobworms, which I duly scattered down that swim. The weather, my notebook says, was on the bright side; water also very bright, a condition of things which did not favour a baiting of lobworms; nor did it favour a beginner in this particular branch of sport, as fine tackle would have to be employed.

We used large quills, that carried ten or a dozen swan shot, and a corking lead, and found we could both swim the stream and long-cork the eddy with them.

In spite of another thousand lobworms that I put in during the day, hour after hour went by, and not a barbel rewarded us. 'Tis true half a dozen chub, several dace, and a score of very fine eels and flounders were landed, and made a goodly show; but the fish we were after came not.

But everything, they say, comes to him who waits, and happening during the late afternoon to go into the osier holt I found a heap of old food rack, that had been washed by a flood into a corner. Under this old heap there were at least fifty of the reddest and liveliest worms that ever I saw, some of them more than three inches long.

As a forlorn hope we tried them, and within the next two hours we landed eleven fish, largest six pounds, smallest two pounds. I got the big one, and I seem to feel him now as he rushed up stream into the very strongest current, and bored, and tugged, and fought on the fine tackle for at least twenty minutes. Ten times I got that float above the water, and nine times he dragged it down again, and dragged and dragged until I thought I should never see it again; but at last I was able to keep the float above the surface, and when this is accomplished the fiercest battle will speedily end.

That catch below Carlton Mill is one of the most cherished recollections of my career; there were only eleven barbel to the two rods, but not one fish was lost and not one broke away from the tackle, the most unusual thing that ever happened to me. I don't think I ever had another catch of barbel in my life where at least one-third of my fish did not come unhooked, after a plunge or two, and escape.

My friend went home with a light heart, a convert to the doctrine I mentioned a page or two back, that barbel fishing, when the fish are on, is a sport of the highest order. But these days are few and far between, even if you make it your special sport, and use tens of thousands of lobworms during a single season.

J. W. Martin, 'The Trent Otter', *My Fishing Days and Fishing Ways*, 1906

Fly Fishing with a Spinning Rod

WHILE ON the subject of dry and wet fly fishing I once caught six trout, all of them curiously enough just under or just over half a pound each, within fifteen minutes, during a four-foot flood the colour of cocoa, using a seven-foot spinning rod, a spinning reel, the finest of lines and of all lures a floating Alder.

It came about this way. I had gone to fish the Tweed for a week in March, hoping to get at least six or seven fish, but on arrival found that the river had grown mightily as a result of warm rain on the high Cheviots and that salmon fishing was hopeless. Becoming either bored or jealous through watching the locals catch endless small and large trout in eddies near the banks, with very long rods and worms of a large size, I seized a spinning rod and some artificial minnows and went to a place near Cornhill where I hoped to touch a trout or two in certain slack corners well out of the current.

When I got to the river I found that there was so much colour that even spinning a minnow offered very little hope of success. While I stood watching this chocolate spate rushing past, I suddenly saw a good trout rise to a fly at the end of a small outward-flowing stream, caused by a tree root which protruded about a yard into the current. The spot where this trout rose was quite ten yards away from the bank and under some low-hanging branches. A pretty hopeless place to cast at even with a fly rod; a seven-foot spinning rod and a thread line did not seem at all the correct weapon for the job. However, I put on a short cast and the only fly I had with me – a floating Alder (which was in my hat) – and tried out a sudden idea which occurred to me.

Somehow, I managed to get my fly and about ten yards of line, all more or less in a heap, onto the current just at the point where it turned sharply from the tree root. After a certain amount of manoeuvring, I managed to straighten the line just as the Alder floated out over the rising trout.

This obliging fish took the fly without the slightest hesitation and was hooked and landed. Thereupon, being rather pleased with myself, I began all over again heaping line and fly by the tree root and allowing it to float out on the current. Again and again I rose and hooked a trout. I caught half a dozen nice trout in quite a short time. My friend the local keeper arrived after I had caught three and was an incredulous witness of the last part of the performance. I was really quite proud of those few small trout, and still am.

George Brennand, *Halcyon*, 1947

Bass Gone Mad

FITFUL GUSTS were coming off land, but for the first part of our journey they troubled us little, as, with all sails set, we glided quickly out of the bay, the wind being dead aft. The bass had been playing havoc with my tackle and I was stowed away in the cuddy of the lugger mounting a Chapman spinner and arranging on it the tail of a mackerel – a capital bait for bass in those waters. I was deeply absorbed in the intricacies of fastening off a piece of whipping with an end all too short, when the little vessel gave a lurch, there was a fearful crash overhead and the cuddy became suddenly darkened. On attempting to grope my way out I found myself shut in by a heap of sailcloth. It was no small accident – the mast had gone overboard. While rounding the rocky headland known as the Monkstone at the end of the bay a tremendous puff of wind had come flying down a gully, hitting the mainsail like a sledgehammer. A splicing in the stay on the windward side slipped, and the mast, having no longer any support, snapped off short. There was a strong current setting in round the point, and all haste was made to get out an anchor.

My crew consisted of a pilot and his nephew. The one a quiet, cautious, and experienced old salt, equal to any emergency; the other, young, active, and willing, and as good a lad as ever sailed in the Bristol Channel.

'If you would come ashore with me, sir,' said the nephew, 'and look after the punt, I will borrow a saw and hatchet and we will be underway again in an hour's time.'

It was good news; for I quite expected this, my last day's bass fishing for the season, would have to be abandoned, as we were five miles from the fishing ground. It was then ten o'clock. The bass fed for about two hours during the strongest run of the flood tide, and if we were not on the spot by one o'clock we should be too late.

While I put Harry ashore and watched over our little punt, for the tide was rising fast, our skipper remained on board, cleared the wreckage, moved the stump of the mast, and got everything ready for his nephew, who, fortunately for us, had served an apprenticeship with a shipbuilder.

He returned in about half an hour's time, and the end of the upper portion of the mast was soon trimmed up and carefully shaped. But it was a difficult task to replace the heavy pole. While Harry and his uncle lifted it, I hauled on to the forestay, and by degrees our stick, as yachtsmen say, pointed once more heavenwards.

An hour later we were heading towards the bass ground, but with one reef down, for the simple reason that our mast was not long enough to carry the whole sail. I returned to the cuddy, finished arranging my tackle, and then took a turn at the helm. After all we arrived at the fishing grounds in good time.

Half a mile from the mainland stands a rocky, treeless, rabbit-haunted island, of a hundred acres or more. During the flood tide a tremendous current sweeps through the channel, and curls and twists, and boils and eddies round the shoals and sandbanks on either side of the fairway.

The local method of fishing is to cruise backwards and forwards across the current, trailing spinning bait, or strip of mackerel, or gurnard skin, or sometimes a whole, but very small, mackerel, called by the fishermen of those parts a 'joey'. The boat must be fast and smartly handled, and, it need hardly be said, there must be a good stiff breeze. None of these essentials were wanting, but owing to our shortened mast we were, as I have said, obliged to keep one reef in the mainsail, which, of course, handicapped us immensely. Worse than this, we were unable to shift our lug when going about, so that on one tack we practically lost about one-third of our sail.

The result was that, whenever the wind fell a little the current caught hold of us, we lost ground, and were about a quarter of an hour in regaining the fishing ground.

As keenly interested in the bass as ourselves were about four or five hundred gulls which were dotted about the cliffs, waiting for the curtain to be raised and the play to commence. Now and then one would launch itself into the air, take a swoop down near the surface of the water, utter a cry, and then fly back again, as if to say, 'No, they have not come yet; you can stay where you are.'

So far the tide had not run very fiercely, and we had no difficulty in holding our own, for there was a good sailing breeze. On one side of the boat, we had out the mackerel-tail bait, spinning splendidly on the Chapman spinner, and on the other the head of a mackerel, with about three inches of skin brought to a point – a bait with which I had landed several fish on various occasions.

Gradually the current became stronger, and little eddies and whirlpools began to form over the sandbanks. Sometimes we were in these and the boat would be twisted round, and almost taken aback before we knew where we were; but we generally managed to keep in the deeper water of the channel, and let our baits play over the edges of the sandbanks. Very soon a yacht joined us, and began cruising over the bass ground – much too large a vessel for the place. One or two other boats from a fishing town sailed up, and five minutes later the fun began.

The gulls saw the fish before we did. Suddenly there was a universal cry from the throats of the birds, and they came dashing down to the water, fighting fiercely with a shoal of bass for the unfortunate herring-fry. Chased by the bass beneath, harried by the gulls above, the poor little fish had a very bad time of it. Our aim and object was to follow the gulls. Wherever they went there we knew were the herring-fry, and wherever herring-fry there also were the bass. It was exciting, and the tackle had to be strong enough to bring them in willy-nilly.

First came a tremendous pull on the mackerel-tail spinning bait, and on hauling in I was disgusted to find two

hooks were broken. Nothing short of a Mahseer hook would do for that fishing.

Harry, who had hold of the line bearing the mackerel head, was more fortunate, and very steadily and quietly hauled in a lovely bass of about three pounds. Then the wind fell somewhat, and just as we were expecting great things we were drawn back into the swirling maelstrom, and, much to our disgust, saw the occupants of all the other boats hauling in fish while we were whirled and twisted about in the boiling waters. My crew did their best, but it was a quarter of an hour or more before we again reached the scene of action. Meanwhile, having prepared another mackerel-tail bait, and fitted up the Chapman spinner with the strongest and largest hooks I had in my box, I was rewarded by bringing another four-pound bass into the boat.

And thus, our sport continued, we could do no wrong and hauled bass aboard like mad things until in an instant it was all over.

John Bickerdyke, *Days of My Life*, 1895

Never Such Luck Again

FOR BEAUTY the lower water could not compare with the upper, being almost destitute of trees, and open to sun and wind. But for interest it might be held superior. The main stream is somewhat swifter, rather deeper, a little narrower. Its fish are, maybe, an ounce or two heavier as a rule and perhaps rather better fed. One remarkable trout, caught almost at the boundary, weighed a pound though it was only twelve inches long, an exceptionally deep, fat fish.

To me, however, the interest of the lower water lay not only in the main stream. Here the meadows are kept pretty constantly irrigated, 'under water' as it is somewhat largely termed, and the result is that there are many carriers and side streams criss-crossed about. In most of these you may find trout, often, too, bigger trout than are commonly caught in the river itself. The older fish of all chalk streams seem to have a tendency to wander into the irrigation channels where no doubt they get very good feeding on minnows, slugs, beetles, and other sustaining things.

To me there is something very fascinating about these outliers, and fishing the carriers is a joy. These carriers are the more amusing because they are so tiny. Getting a three-quarter-pound trout out of a runnel two feet wide and eighteen inches deep is the queerest adventure.

It is not orthodox fishing as a rule, for the fish seldom rise – there is no hatch of fly to speak of. But deft casting in the likely spots will often fetch up a fish whose existence was only hypothetical.

One day in one of these carriers I saw what looked like a dimple under a dock leaf. I put a ginger quill on the place, had an immediate rise, and then for about five minutes walked solemnly up and down in attendance on the biggest trout I ever hooked on the fishery. He never hurried himself, but cruised to and fro, and in the end the fly came away just as I was wondering whether it would be a matter for the taxidermist. I think that trout was a two-pounder, though, of course, estimates of lost fish are suspect by general consent, and it does not do to be rash. Anyhow, I can say without hesitation that I was filled with grief that bordered on despair. But all was not lost and I determined to soldier on.

One of the two biggest fish I caught during that season was the result of long-continued efforts on a little side stream which joins the river near the ford.

Near the point of the junction it is quite considerable, though almost without current. Here big trees shade it from the sun nearly all day, tall rushes grow along the bank, and the trout cruise about in droves lazily sucking in gnats, spinners

and other trifles, and occasionally splashing at the sedges which are tempted out by the subdued light.

There are a couple of hundred yards of this still water, and one can easily spend a morning here peeping through the rushes and occasionally dropping a fly in front of a fish which comes within reach – they patrol the place like peaceful pickets. On a very hot day this waiting game is to be commended, and a brace of trout may be caught without too much hard labour.

Ordinarily the fish are no bigger than those elsewhere in the fishery, but one day I became aware of a mighty one which smacked great jaws as he fed, and made great commotions as he moved about.

Presently I saw him, and he had fifteen or sixteen inches to his credit. And then I rose him and hooked him; the water heaved as he rolled over, and the fly came away. For several weekends I pursued that fish in vain. He was sometimes in one place, sometimes in another. Occasionally he would make a pretence of rising, but he would never really take a fly again till a day nearly at the end of July, when I overcame his caution by a trick which was probably very wrong. I put on a fly with a long straggling hackle and placed it before him. He came, looked, mocked, and went away.

I withdrew the fly and waited for some minutes till he returned on his beat. Then I cast it in front of him and as he came to look again twitched the point of the rod ever so slightly. The fly waggled on the water, the fish perceived that there was something which had life and movement, opened his jaws wide, closed them and in due course weighed a splendid one pound three ounces.

And so it continued. Those fish demanded nothing finicking in the way of flies, but were satisfied with a substantial orange quill on a No. 2 hook. After the first misadventure I think I landed every trout that took the fly except the very last, which got off in the dusk through being held too hard. I had four brace averaging over one and three-quarter pounds, and they fought so fiercely that playing and landing them literally occupied nearly the whole time; there were very short intervals between landing one and hooking the next.

I do not suppose I shall ever have such an evening again. Very seldom indeed would it happen that the fish were in a taking mood for long enough to make such a wonderful basket a possibility.

H. T. Sheringham, Trout Fishing Memories and Morals, 1920

New Rod, First Salmon

OVER THE brown moor under a sullen sky, which had a damp, misty look, as of rain clouds not long departed – squish, squash, through the peaty mire we trudged, a piscatorial Pylades and Orestes, so far as a love of the art which we practised in common went; my companion was Jock Coulter, the village cobbler, one of the best and keenest brothers of the angle I have ever met. Poor Jock! he has long since gone to his long rest beneath the old yew tree in the old kirkyard, beside the Whammle-burn, which in life he loved to wander by so well. From the first thread and pin of the infant angler Jock had trained my early efforts up to the capture of a noble burn trout of two ounces; and many a dozen, many a score of dozens, of much larger burn trout had Jock and I deluded by various means in company; and when the sea trout came up the Whammle, many a fine and lively two- and three-pounder had I succeeded in bagging under Jock's able guidance.

But today there was more important game afoot.

Today I came of age from an angling point of view, for I bore upon my shoulder a brand new salmon rod, presented to me by a wealthy uncle, lately returned from shaking the

pagoda tree in Eastern climes. It was a lovely little Forest rod but despised by Jock.

'To sleep, perchance to dream,' says Hamlet.

Hamlet was not a fisherman that I am aware of, though he knew Polonius for a fishmonger. But to sleep without dreaming that night was impossible for me. What terrific single combats I fought with monster salmon, perfect krakens, and how I woke, so to speak, with my line broken and salmon gone, again and again, till about six o'clock, when a handful of gravel at my windowpane awoke me to the sense that Jock awaited me below. How I dressed that morning I never remember, but everything went on the wrong way, and had to be reversed, and, like Ebenezer Scrooge, I made, 'a Laocoön of myself with my stockings'. Never mind; they were properly applied at last, and down I went, and snatching a hasty cup of milk in one hand and a pile of buttered oatcake in the other, I made the briefest breakfast which I ever did. Then seizing the rod and reel from the corner where I had placed them, I sallied out to join Jock. How well I remember everything that morning! I with the rod, Jock wielding the net as his insignia of office, as we left the gate.

The morning was misty from showers overnight. The sun had made no way in the heavens as yet, and the laverock (the lark) which usually sprang aloft from the meadows at this hour to meet him, was silent. The rowans and the birches were weeping for his absence as we broke away from the cultivated land out on to the broad brown moor, for the glory of the heather was not yet. I can see now the glistening pools of black peat water and the grey boulders scattered erratically about, with snags of silver-barked birch, thousands of years old, and superior to age apparently, which made startling contrast where the labours of the peat cutter had thrown them aside. Ben Vrackie, enveloped in mist, was only visible as to its lower slopes.

There was nothing moving on the moor save a far-off shepherd and his collie looking for a stray sheep, and they marched with heads bent down, as though the morning had damped even their seasoned natures.

As yet the pipe of curlew and the whistle of plover was silent.

'It'll be a braw morning for the fashing!' said Jock. 'She'll be in graun ply, and I'd no wunner but ye got a fusshe, or even twa.'

Another hundred yards or so, and a dull, rushing noise met our ear. 'Mon, yere in luck, she's ower the stepping stones I'm thinking, and if sae ye're sure of sport.'

In a few more minutes we came upon the river, a moderate-sized salmon stream, spread out and shallow just here, with a range of big stepping stones, which ran across the ford, but of which little could be seen now, as the water was rushing over them tumultuously. Nasty, dangerous stones they were, too, at times, and more than one person had been drowned in trying to pass them in flood; but we couldn't afford a bridge then, and had to put up with the stones, or go five miles round. While I put the rod together, Jock rigged up the cast and looped it on, and then we proceeded a few hundred yards beyond the flat to Whammle-foot, a fine swirly salmon cast, where Whammle fell into the Doughty. Taking my stand on a convenient strand, I reeled off a dozen yards of line and commenced casting. For some throws nothing came of it.

At length, I cast towards a point where a big stone could just be seen under water.

'Canny, Geordie, canny!' said my companion. 'If there's a fusshe in a' the river, it is there.' And just as my fly swept over the stone a great boil and swirl rose immediately under it, and a, 'There he is,' from Jock, as I struck upwards sharply and instantaneously.

'Hey, mon, mon! Ye just pu'd the fee clean awa frae him. Had ye let it bide in the watter he'd have had a taste o it, for certain. Mind, now, it's a gowden rule when ye see a saumon rise, count three before ye strike, an' if ye dinna fell a rug o him by then ye needna strike at a'.'

Very good advice possibly, but utterly futile to a keen youngster on his first salmon. We rested the fish a few minutes, and tried him again, but he was sulky at having his breakfast offered to him, and then pulled away again, and would have nothing more to say to us. I fished on down to the end of the cast and got a dashing rise, but I found it was only a big trout. I was disappointed and yet, when trout fishing, I had tried that particular trout most carefully with a variety of flies over and over again, for I knew him well, and many a time my heart had been in my mouth as he came up cautiously and critically inspected my fly or minnow, and then, with a wave of his tail, expressive of his contempt for it, retreated to his watery fastness. But today, because I chanced to be after salmon, I looked on him as inferior ware, while he, who had so cautiously examined into moderate offers and reasonable four or five per cent investments where he had a fair chance of getting off with bait and all for a scrape, like a rash speculator, thinking he could realise ten or fifteen per cent, with limited liability, risked his all-in-one mad rush and lost it.

Verily the world of fishes may be likened unto that of humanity in many respects.

After this we went on up the river until we came to a very fine stream, called the Spinning Wheel – next to it in high water was always visible a huge eddy. The fish, if they took at all, usually took on the outside edge of this eddy, where the water was thinner than in the middle of it, and you had apparently to cast up stream instead of down, in consequence of the eddy. All this had been explained to me by my mentor as we came up to it, and I made my casts as well as I could, though perhaps not with all the skill of a master, for once or twice the line got into the eddy, which partly drowned the fly. But this, as it happened, did me no disservice, for, as I pulled the fly out of it once, I felt a pluck, and I gave an answering stroke, thinking it was possibly a small trout, and the next moment my reel was whirling and screaming like a circular saw, for a salmon had taken the fly deep under water, and made no break on the surface.

'Mon, ye're on him, and ye'll see a ploy the noo,' shouted Jock, in great excitement.

Down into the deep eddy plunged the heavy fish, taking out line rapidly, while my rod was bent into that delightful arch which is the most beautiful of all curves to the angler's eye.

'Move up, move up, or he'll droon the line in the eddy,' said Jock, taking me by the arm like a policeman, and urging me up the stream, and I should have been in a difficulty, but just then the fish came up to the surface above the eddy and made a tremendous leap in the air, thus helping me to get the line straight again. What a glorious sight it was to see that noble fish, a good twelve-pounder, springing out of his native element to seek refuge in another, and coming down with a splash that made my blood tingle and my heart beat! Then he took a violent rush downstream on the further side of the eddy, and once more the reel discoursed delicious music.

'Ye'll hae him full surely,' said Jock, 'for it's a fine deep water, and there's nae obstructions.'

For several minutes the fine fellow made frantic rushes up and down, but as I wound him in after each they grew shorter and shorter, and I felt I was becoming rapidly his master. My excitement was aesthetic, intense.

To all languid, placid natures, if you want to feel too, too utterly utter, I say, hook your first salmon, and if you want to penetrate the depths of despair, lose him.

'Lead him in to that strand, Master Geordie,' said Jock, as the fish rolled over on his side and gave a heavy but futile plunge. I did so, and Jock, standing knee-deep with extended net, waited till I drew the salmon within reach. Slowly and with extreme caution, supine on his side, I drew him nearer and nearer. There was a short, quick stroke, and *Salmo salar*, in all his silver armour, was dragged, flapping violently, up over

the yellow sands as we made the rocks echo with a lusty cheer, whereat suddenly Ben Vrackie came out of the mist, as if to see what was the matter.

For at that moment the sun, which had long been battling with the clouds for supremacy, broke through and dispersed them, and bathed us in a golden light, as if to celebrate the auspicious occasion.

Francis Francis, Angling Reminiscences, 1887

Better Wild Than Stocked

THE GREAT thing – perhaps the greatest thing of all – about fishing (which sounds like a trawler is involved) or angling (which sounds like Izaak Walton is involved) is the constant element of surprise.

One minute all is quiet; the fly fisherman silently throws his line upstream again and again and nothing happens. The coarse fisherman sits still as a heron on his basket, so still that often a bird, even a kingfisher, will land momentarily on the tip of his rod. Yet nothing happens. Then suddenly as fast as electricity, lightning reflexes are demanded, all is action and fierce intense concentration as a fish takes.

It has too often been said by those who do not fish that they would not have the patience for fishing. Here is the biggest misunderstanding. Fishing is not about patience; it is about controlled impatience. The apparently calm and serene angler is actually in a state of permanent tension, coiled like a spring waiting for that tiny pluck on the line or the savage take that changes everything in an instant.

Then there is the bittersweet pleasure of contrasting days, unpredictable days. All the omens – weather, tackle, time of year and venue – may be propitious for a great day and yet disaster, or at least a blank, follows. On another day all the omens are poor and yet the angler enjoys a day of success that he will remember for the rest of his life.

And anglers are all different and all pleased in different ways. I recall fishing one of the finest beats on the Test, but it was dull fishing, the river stocked with too many big fish that were too easily taken. It was horribly commercial, a big company that owned the stretch simply trying to make as much money as possible from tourists and beginners. Overstocking the river with big fish kept the customers happy, but the whole set up was just an embarrassment and a very poor advertisement for fishing.

On that stretch of the Test I caught five trout one after another and each weighing more than three pounds, but could not count it a great day. It was like fishing in one's garden pond for one's pet carp.

Two days later I had a morning on the Lower Thames, a river still dirty, its banks still lined with the remnants of a commercial, an industrial past. I had very few hopes of a decent fish, but it was exciting to be on a big river where the fish were as wild as fish could still be in the modern world and in a small crowded over-polluted island.

My float drifted down the steady current for perhaps the hundredth time and then dipped gently beneath the green water. I lifted the rod and felt that indescribably exciting throb as a good fish plunged out into the current.

Here the excitement was boosted by one simple fact – I had no idea what had taken my bait. A moment later there was a swirl and my fish came to the surface: it was a roach and an absolute beauty. I was convinced it must be a two-pounder, a specimen I had longed to catch for thirty years and more. Slowly the fish came towards my net; it was bigger even than I had at first suspected. Then inches from success, disaster. The rod straightened, the hook flew into the air and I watched as my huge roach rolled over and disappeared.

I felt like throwing rod, reel, line and basket into the river and swearing off fishing forever. A full ten minutes it took to recover, at least partly, from my disappointment.

I reasoned thus: roach are shoal fish and shoals tend to contain fish of a similar size. I began casting again but convinced that I had talked myself into believing the impossible. I could not possibly hook another roach as big as that lost and wonderful fish. Yet on that very first cast the impossible happened. The float dipped in just the place where it had dipped before. I felt the lunge and the pull and the fearful excitement. I played that fish as if my life depended on it and when it was finally in the net, I experienced a level of joy that comes only very rarely in life.

And what did that red-fin weigh? Well, the gods were on my side, for that roach weighed exactly one ounce over the magic two-pound mark. It was truly the fish of a lifetime and better far than those dull, fat (and expensive) farm-bred trout dumped into what was once one of the world's most wonderful rivers.

Martin Giles, *Angling*, 1980